CAUGHT

CAUGHT

Annetta Caldwell

Copyright © 2025 Annetta Caldwell

All Rights Reserved

The stories in this book reflect the author's recollection of events. Some names, locations, and identifying characteristics have been changed.

Any unauthorized reprint or use of this material is prohibited without express written permission from the author and/or publisher.

Scripture quotations marked NIV are taken from the Holy Bible, New International Version, copyright © 1973, 1978, 1984 by International Bible Society.

Cover art by

John Martindale

Published by Lemonade Stand Press

ISBN: 979-8-218-68309-2

Version 1.2 – August 2025

Dedicated first to Jesus, who is everything to me, my amazing husband, Ryan, for all your support, my awesome kids, and my dear friends, who all encouraged and prayed for me.

Table of Contents

1. -The Dark- — 1
2. -Loss of Innocence- — 4
3. -The Chase- — 7
4. -A Glimmer of Light- — 15
5. -An Unforgettable Birthday- — 18
6. -Steal Much? - — 24
7. -Hole in My Heart Looking to Fill- — 28
8. -Multiple Identities- — 32
9. -A Narrow Escape- — 36
10. -Spiraling Yet Hope Calling- — 38
11. -Inconsequential? - — 43
12. -A Downward Tunnel with a Sight of Light- — 45
13. -A Deadly Plunge- — 49
14. -A New Beginning- — 56
15. -A Long Road Ahead- — 60
16. -An Unlikely Encounter- — 63
17. -Steps Taken, Steps Lost- — 68
18. -Look Up- — 72
19. -This New Life- — 76
20. -The Spoils- — 79
21. -Things Given, Things Taken- — 82
22. -Fight, Flight, Run- — 84
23. -Cult? - — 87
24. -The Start of Something New- — 92
25. -Almost Stopped- — 101
26. -Forgiveness- — 104
27. -Say Hello, Say Goodbye- — 107
28. -The Start- — 111
29. -Thailand- — 116
30. -Jumping despite- — 120

31. -Match-Maker-	125
32. -Unexpected Blessings-	131
33. -The Aftermath-	134
34. -Jesus, My Everything-	141
35. -Love Restore All Things-	145
36. -Hurt Again-	152
37. -The Big Day and Beyond-	158
38. -Back on the Road and a Little Surprise-	167
39. -Back on the Road, Take Two-	172
40. -Shock-	177
41. -Rainbows After Storms-	180
42. -Hardship with Grace-	184
43. -Good News-	187
44. -Hurry Up and Slow Down-	192
45. -Foe or Friend-	196
46. -Pain, Pain, Joy-	206
47. -Overwhelm, Fear, Surprise-	213
48. -A Rollercoaster-	219
49. -The Big Day-	224
50. -Space More Space-	229
51. -Joy, Joy Freedom-	236
52. -Stepping Out and Dancing-	247
53. -In the Waiting, God is Healing-	253
54. -Failed Dreams-	260
55. -Unexpected-	265
56. -Beauty from Ashes-	273
57. -Deliverance-	288
58. -Lemonade, Anyone? -	298
59. -But Wait, There's More-	309
60. -The Good, the Bad, and the Scary - Part 1-	320
61. -The Good, the Bad, and the Scary - Part 2-	333

Chapter 1

-The Dark-

I drank his blood.

Cars are everywhere. Horns are blaring, and it's packed, and everyone is busy. I am right in the middle of the nightlife. Billy, Stephanie, and I are talking about witchcraft and drinking blood the other night. An awful thought goes through my head: why not drink a stranger's blood? Looking around, I can't think straight. The screeching of tires and yelling from pedestrians distracts me until I see him. His dark hair flows in the wind, and a leather brown jacket sits on his motorcycle. That's him.

I ask him if I could drink his blood, and he says Sure, without a care in the world, and pulls out a knife and cuts his arm. I begin drinking his blood right on the spot. What just happened? Why did I choose him? I don't know. Something just drew me to him. I feel numb and yet confused. The world is standing still. What have I done? I knew I went too far. I feel instant regret. Why am I doing this, as his blood is still on my mouth? I feel like I am in a nightmare that won't end. It seems the farther into darkness I go, the worse I feel. Why can't I be free?

Just days before this, when I was with Stephanie and Billie. We were talking about spells. There are good witches and bad witches, she explained. We were reading about the spells and how we could do things. Have power. We could make things happen. It sounded good to me. The more we talked, the more we realized the power of these spells came with drinking other people's blood. The thought sounded scary, bizarre, and risky. But I wanted to try it. Maybe this could help me. Maybe this is the answer I have been looking for to help with my life.

I think I can fight darkness with more darkness. So, although Billy thought it was strange, he said Ok, let's do it. As we cut each other's arms, it was a surreal feeling. As I went to each of my friends' arms and we cut each other, it was as if I were watching a movie. There is pain for a second, but my adrenaline is pumping. The room is swirling with darkness.

I begin to taste his blood, and he tastes mine, and then we switch, and my friend Stephanie does the same. It's hypnotic and nauseating at the same time. It's like something awakened in me that was heavy and fear-binding. I know deep inside it's wrong, but by this point in my life, my conscience is so scarred it's hard to know if I could trust what was right and wrong.

After we finish, I am connected to my friends in a way that I am not connected to anyone else. And now it's like Satan has full access to me. The path I am on has no light, and everything is clouded with shame for what I am doing. My life has been anything but perfect and fine growing up. And there were reasons I was in the mess I was in now. Let me take you there.

Chapter 2
-Loss of Innocence-

I safely tuck myself in bed. It's dark and dreary feeling. All of a sudden, I hear yelling in the background. It's happening more and more. I just cover my ears and pray I can just not hear anymore. Then finally the house is quiet again. Then I hear that sound. The door creaks open.

It's late, but I know what is coming. It is a familiar feeling. He comes into my room almost every night. I am trying to pretend I am somewhere else. Anywhere but here. I feel like I am not in my own body anymore. I hear and feel things happening. It's more than my mind can comprehend. I can scream, "Stop!" but nothing is coming out of my mouth. My innocence is being taken away again and more every time he comes into my room.

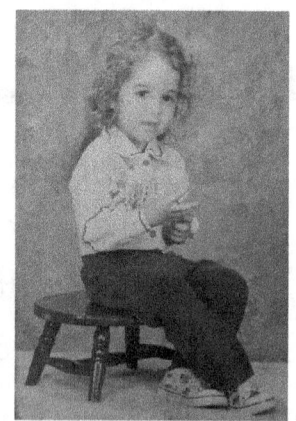

Finally, he leaves, and I feel relieved. What have I done? Why is this happening? I have to go to school now, but I feel so alone, hurt, and ashamed.

What if someone knows about what happened? Would they take them away? What are others thinking of me? Do they see what happens every night? Will they think I am gross, dirty, and damaged? My friends think I am stained. It's like someone wrote with a marker, damaged, worthless, shameful. Every day, I am trying to hide it. Sometimes I just want to hide at my friends' houses. They don't have problems like I do.

My new friend, Linda, found her dad's liquor cabinet. "Let's try it," she says with a boldness in her voice. I am scared, but would love to try something new and exciting. Though we are only in the 5th grade, it doesn't matter, I am big enough to handle this. The first sip enters my mouth. Wow, I feel excited and daring. Yes. Somehow, this fits. Why haven't I done this before?

Then next weekend I say, "let's do it again", though it tastes disgusting. I welcome any distraction with everything going on. Now, even though I am super young, I know there is something wrong with drinking this. Haunting me, I keep it all in the back of my head.

Chapter 3
-The Chase-

Max took an interest in me. He's one of the popular kids. The most popular girls, Jane and Lisa, said Max liked me. Max is not my type. He's super short and not very attractive. He has an entourage of guys who look like his bodyguards. Even though I do not like him, this is my chance to get into the in crowd. I play along, acting like I like him -- even though I don't. I just want people to like me. I am so excited! I got invited to a party and I will be with the cool kids, the only issue? I must pretend to like Max.

The day of the party is finally here! I am so excited. What should I wear? I know my best outfit that I just bought! Oh, my goodness, it happened so fast. I see Linda. Hey! What should I say? Act cool, Annetta. Act cool. Hi! I am so happy you invited me.

Linda seems to really like me. I can't believe I am at the most popular girl's house! Ding dong! Oh wow. I remember that girl, Taylor. Hey! I hope I don't sound dumb. Ok. I will just sit here and try to act calmly. What am I doing? I don't even like Max.

What if they can tell? Knock, knock! Max will be here at any moment! The door opens. Tension is filling the room. There's a gasp in the air. Max makes his grand entrance, "I'm heeeeerrrrre!" Oh my gosh! Is this happening? Am I really the center of attention? My head feels hazy. Am I in a movie or what?

"There she is," someone said, bringing everyone's attention to me. It's a huge moment for me—like time has frozen, and I am the center of attention. I smile, muster up all the confidence I have, and sweetly say, "Hey, Max." He smiles back, cocky as ever, and asks, "Will you go out with me? "Even though I didn't like him, I said, "Yes." Suddenly, everyone starts clapping and cheering. Applause fills the room, and I am surrounded by the popular kids. For the first time, I feel like I truly belong. This was the feeling I had longed for.

For about an hour, I bask in my newfound popularity and love the attention that being with Max brings me. But deep down, I don't really like him. Secretly, I like one of his friends who came in with him. Max and I share a very awkward kiss, and while everything seems to be going great with my new friends, I struggle to pretend that I want to be Max's girlfriend.

During the party, the uneasiness grows since I know I am being dishonest. Can anyone see the look on my face? I don't hide my emotions very well. The room is getting closed up. Panic, coupled with guilt, is engulfing me. I have to say something. Where is Lisa? After an hour, I pull her aside in a room. Quickly, I tear the band-aid, hoping judgment won't be too severe. As the words come off my tongue, the look of shock and disbelief is on Lisa's face. Maybe I should have kept quiet. But it's too late now. She looks at me and says that I should have said something. Now, honesty is my only option. Though I hope Lisa understands, her body language and tone speak something totally different.

I inch towards the door, after what seems like hours, and turn the handle with shaky hands. It's time. Be brave, Annetta, I tell myself. Max is standing with his friends with a happy glow. He introduces me again as his girlfriend. The night can't get away from me. I have to say something as Lisa glares at me from across the room. "Max, I gently say, "Can I talk to you? he says, "sure, with a playful look in his eyes.

He walks with me to the room with an arm around me. The words were coming like molasses off my tongue. Max, I want to break up. I don't like you like this, and I need to be honest. I am so sorry; I say with guilt pulsing through every word. His eyes show hurt and disbelief. "You lied to me?" He knows it. I can see it. He knows I used him for his gift of popularity. He rushes out of the room to tell his friends.

As I exit the room, all around me, people are whispering. And judgment is piercing my heart deep in my soul. As I turn around the room, Lisa, whom I confided in, makes an announcement. Hey everyone, Annetta decided to break up with Max. She reveals my intentions. Even more whispering is happening. Everyone decides to either leave or take the party outside. I look at Lisa and tell her I will stay inside. She glares at me, with a reprisal in her smile, "I think that's a good decision to stay in here."

I feel like an outcast and a vulnerability that I have never felt with a friend group. I gather my things, and though I can hear laughing and the life of a party outside, I find a place to sleep on the couch. I place my head on the pillow, second-guessing everything that happened just twenty minutes ago. Regret, remorse, and panic are my companions tonight. My sleep is nauseating.

Turns and twists all night, I am replaying the scene in my head. Maybe I should not have been honest with Max. I could have pretended to like him a little longer than an hour. Finally, morning comes. Wait, I can't move my fingers. My toes won't move either. Panic is encompassing me. As I look down, I see it. Super glue!

My hands and toes are superglued, along with my new pants. Everything is ruined, and no one is in sight. All my friends are gone. A sense of fear and humiliation hit me. Who did this? I can guess it was Lisa, and everyone at the party. Revenge. It hits you hard when it is against you. When you participate in it, it feels like justice. Neither is good. I gather my belongings with my head down. My inside matches my outside now.

Worn, torn, and broken. My desire for acceptance has left me alone. And with nowhere to turn to. I call my mom to pick me up, face the consequences, and tell her what my new friends just did, but I don't tell her what I did last night. Shame is a heavy dress to wear.

The next day, my friend Linda wants to hang out, but I don't know why. She embraces me back even though I have blown off our plans together. She is upset but forgives me. I hang up the phone, and we meet at the ice-skating rink. As I share my pain and mistakes, a horrible idea pops into my head. I somehow have Max's friend's number with me. I think he gave it to me to help me reach Max at some point. My friend Linda questions my sanity. "Girl, don't call and ask for his friend!

My heart races with anticipation. I type in the number with shaky hands. As Turner answers, I invite him to ice skating and ask if he wants to go out with me. My judgment is clouded with hurt and a desire to be loved. His words came quickly and sharply. Yes, I will go out with you. Let me just call you back in an hour. As the phone rings an hour later, I hear the words, "I'm breaking up with you; that's what you get for breaking up with my friend Max." I deserve that. The drama quickly unfolds as I return to school on Monday. Consequences speak louder than words.

I pack my bag and lunch. The mundane tasks comfort me. What should I wear? Does it matter? Today, I will be the laughingstock. But how bad would it be? Only time will tell. As I entered the dreary hallway, it happens. I see the kids pointing at me. Laughing at me. Maybe they heard the story of my hands and toes being super-glued. Maybe the rumors have already begun to fly around the campus. Either way, I was here. And the dreaded moment came. I look and there they are. Lisa, Max, and all the popular kids. Max won't make eye contact, but I hear their whispers and laughter.

I think I see his friend, Turner. My face turns white, then red, and all I know is I must get out of this hallway. The lockers are closing in on me. I can't find an escape. I go into the lunchroom, and Linda is there. It happens to be my birthday, and she hands me a balloon. I don't deserve a friend like her. I'm so sorry that I left you and cancelled our plans. "Annetta, I forgive you, but you must stop chasing popularity. Be yourself. There will always be friends who like you for you." I look at her with tear-stained eyes, I humiliated myself and messed up big this time." I know you did, but it's time to move on.

Chapter 4
-A Glimmer of Light-

Linda and I are fighting again. She can see through me. I don't want to just be like everyone else. She looks at me through walls she has built up. Maybe I betrayed her one too many times. I head home and see my brother skating on the street. He is so carefree. He doesn't care what anyone thinks. I want to be like him. I am so tired of my desire for popularity. Maybe I can just stop caring. I borrow his skateboard and begin learning.

I walk through the halls weeks after the event with the popular group, and I see them. Twins! "Hey, are you new here?" "Yes, I'm Rita, and this is Tori." I guess you heard about me," I say sheepishly. "Yes, but no worries. We don't care what the Preppies and the bougie think. Why not hang with us? We won't judge you. You don't need them." What is this feeling I have? I feel comfortable. I feel warm and loved on the inside. Is this what acceptance feels like?

Tori and Rita, and I are getting close. I am changing, but was I changing for the better? I dye my hair black and buy my skateboard. I am actually good at this. One day, as I am enjoying my new look, short jean shorts, a strong flowing flannel around my thin waist, a skintight shirt, and jet-black hair, holding a new skateboard, I catch the eye of Ricky. Everywhere he goes, people know who he is. He wears a new leather jacket and carries himself differently. He has shoulder-length blond hair and a confident smile that can make any girl blush.

Ricky's friend finds me in the hurried hallway at school and approaches me, "Hey, my friend Ricky was wondering if you would be interested in going out." Okay, Annetta, keep your cool. My chest is tight with anticipation. Doesn't he know what I have done? Why would he want me? He's popular too, just with a different crowd. I am stuck in my own thoughts. I manage to lift my head ever so slightly. The words fall flat. "Okay, sure, I would like that."

Oh my gosh. Did I just say that out loud? I feel so dumb. He looks at me excitedly and says Great, I will let him know! What have I done? My heart is beating so fast. What if this is a repeat of the last guy? What if he ends up embarrassing himself in front of everyone? I can't take another rejection.

Regardless, I already said yes, I can't change that now. I look around for my new friends. Tori and Rita are walking alone, feeling the boredom of school. I break up the monotony with my words. Oh my gosh, guess who asked me out? As the words were coming off my tongue, Rita gives me the side eye. Jealousy was dripping off every look she gives me. Tori manages a smile and says, "Great!" Deep inside, I know neither is happy for me. I can feel it, but the excitement overpowers the worry of what they think. My birthday is this weekend, so for now, Ricky will have to wait.

Chapter 5
-An Unforgettable Birthday-

Preparations are being made for my 8th grade party. Cake is bought, minimal decorations bought and a frantic cleaning of the house. The thoughts are racing through my head. Will anyone show up? I have invited so many people, but would anyone still want to hang out with me? Though things have died down at school, I still feel the effects of the rejection. Does anyone really want to celebrate with me? The house is still a mess, and I feel embarrassed at the thought of people showing up here. I yell at my mom out of feeling flustered.

She is trying to comfort me. "Annetta, it will be ok. I am sure friends will show up." Soon after her words fall on deaf ears, there is a sound that is sweet to my ears: the doorbell. Suddenly, friends come fluttering in with presents and joy in their voices. Could it be? I have people showing up. Tori and Rita arrive, along with some friends from school. Let's cut the cake and have ice cream and presents! Childhood joy is coming to the surface. The joy I am feeling can't be stopped. I think I am healing. I am feeling love. My family seems normal. No one knows about anything yet.

We go outside for some fresh air. Who is that? Tori and Rita squeal with delight. It's Olivia! Olivia catches the eyes of everyone. Her outfit is flowy, and she walks with an unusual shuffle. She seems older than middle school. Maybe it's the darkness in her steps or how her hair is dishevelled.

She winks at me in a curious way. Are you ready for the party to start? We huddle into the living room, and she opens her sash of tarot cards. The darkness fills the room. Curiosity takes hold of me. I already know about Ouija boards from parties I went to. It was exciting for me. But this, this is different. I can feel darkness swirling all around me. It's your turn, Annetta. Let's see what I find out about you. My heart is racing. I know this is wrong, but I still allow myself to go in.

It's like another world. She finishes telling me about the cards as she flips this animal card over and then another. It's like curses she is speaking over me. And I am not fighting it. I feel different. Fear is near. It has a fragrance. It smells foul and tormenting. I regret opening this door. And as thoughts are pouring into my head, I hear her call out, Next...

As each girl tries these cards, more darkness enters the room. Fear exudes from each girl's eyes. They match mine; I am sure. The torment we all feel is seen in each other as we look back and forth at each other. Olivia knows what she is doing. She is experienced. She has now exhilarated her tormentor, as more have joined his dark tribe.

Then I hear these words, "do you want to go deeper? Darker?" I whisper a frightened yes. And as quickly as I say it, the room is exploding with more things to do. Do you have a bible? We will go into another dimension. A friend tears up, I think maybe we shouldn't go that far. Girls begin to regret what they are doing. Some are curious enough to try it. The other girls want to leave, and so parents come to pick up their kids.

I can't escape the next level of witchcraft. I grab the bible with shivers going down my spine and begin to rub and move it with the satanic book. I feel a shift. Now she, Olivia, looks at me and with a crooked smile says, "that's right." She tells me what to say. I know they are sinister. "You must be the one doing it." Her voice is now no longer friendly but demanding and mean. I drop the Bible and the satanic book. I can't do it anymore. My hands are shaking, and fear is choking the life out of me. Olivia, Tori, and Rita decide it's time to leave. Only a couple of girls decide to stay the night.

Maybe we can put all this behind us and just get ready for the night. As I look around, the remaining girls go to my room. My poster looks strange. Is it coming alive? The guy on the poster appears to be moving. Is it my imagination? Panic is in the air like electricity charging through a broken socket. I run to the other room; my friends Callie and Brittney are still processing everything.

Hey, can you guys come here and look at the poster? They look, and yes, they see the same thing. The poster appears to be talking. Callie yells, "I am sleeping in your living room! I am not sleeping in your room!" We all run out crying and screaming. My older sister stops me. "Annetta, it's not real. Calm down." She tries to comfort me, but deep in my heart, I know it is real, and I am not ok.

Chapter 6
-Steal Much? -

Tilly, my other friend is a wild one. I think I am attracting all the wrong people. She is nice, but she shoplifts a lot. She loves to hang out with strange guys, and I feel I am just along for the ride most of the time. "Hey, want to go on an adventure with me? They have so many cute clothes and things at the mall. Let's walk there, and then we can catch the bus home." Walking along the highway, I was scared. Cars are honking as they drive by, and we are wearing just swimsuits. Please, please keep us safe, I think to myself, maybe even saying a prayer with each honk. Finally, we make it up a long hill, and then we get big, beautiful bags as we enter the mall.

She looks at me with dangerous eyes and says to start putting anything I want in my bag. I see some perfume I like, and I put it in my oversized bag. "Today is your day. You can get whatever you want." She says with a giggle of glee. "You mean whatever I want?" Clothes, jewelry, and everything seems amazing. I peek in a clothing store. Oh my gosh, they have the cutest clothes! I begin talking to the worker. "Hey, do you think I could find a different size? Can you help me with putting this on?"

I keep asking questions and distracting her as my friend is putting clothes under her other clothes, and I do the same. As I am sheepishly moving slowly to the door, I yell a friendly thank you. Guilt is an unwelcome guest but is still following me as I exit the store. When we start for the door, I feel exhilarated and scared. The door is big and open. "We made it!", I shout to my friend. The painful awareness hits both of us. The bus stop is on the other side of the mall, and we have way too much to carry.

"Are you sure we should go back in?" Tilly was adamant. "We must go back and catch the bus. You don't want to walk all the way home with all this stuff, do you?" "No, I don't", I say sheepishly. So, I reluctantly follow her. As we take heavy, slow steps in, I exhale slowly as I feel a hand on my shoulder actually a big, heavy hand. Fear grips me as I look at the angry, concerned officer. As he begins questioning us, I can't think straight.

The room is spinning as the handcuffs are placed on my hands. What have I done? As we are walking, shame is hanging on me like a heavy chain. As panic sets in the walls are becoming thick and heavy. My breath is heavy, and my heart is racing. We enter the police car, reality hitting both of us. We make our way into the sordid, isolated building. I have never been to Juvie before. As I look around, panic fills my eyes, "Tilly, we have to get out of here!" I tell all the kids around me, "Let's try to escape!" In my feeble attempt, I grab a chair and throw it at the glass in hopes of escaping! It only bounces off the durable glass. In my embarrassment, I slink down waiting for my turn to face my mom.

The look in my mom's eyes cut so deep. "I am sorry, Mom" is all I can muster up. But the damage is done, the disappointment is here, and the consequences cannot be removed. A week later, the court is here, and I bring my trembling body in, with the judge's words echoing loudly, community service, and I know what is done is done, no going back.

Chapter 7
-Hole in My Heart Looking to Fill-

Here I am starting high school, and my heart is so broken. I sit and look at the trees and nature and find comfort there. I am trying not to use drugs, though alcohol has been helping me some. I feel the stares of everyone judging me. I know I am dressed in all black with black mascara and eye liner. I just feel it matches my heart, deep, dark and depressed. I find a razor blade. Just a cut won't hurt. Just a cut here or a cut there. It seems to take the edge off. I hate myself so much. Why am I even here. Maybe I should just die. Everyone hates me. My family hates me. I hate me.

As people throw things at me and call me a freak, I believe them. Maybe I am a freak. As I am looking at the tree in front of me and crying, I think, I am worthless, a guy Roger puts his hand in front of me. I look up at him. He says, "if you come with me and my friends, I have something that might make you feel better."

As I walk behind my new friend, I feel hope for a brief moment. The steps towards what I think would bring me freedom are just more shackles on my feet. As I near the broken fence, I see them. My new friends. All dressed in Emo, they exude hurt and trauma. With smiles on their faces, the drugs are placed in front of me, "just try this and you will feel so much better."

From the moment the drugs enter my body, they are right. I felt the pain dissipating. As I get higher and higher, it's like reality is disappearing. And now I have my answer. These new friends and these new drugs are just what I have been searching for. No more pain, no more fear, just freedom. But there is always a cost. Always something or someone that must pay the price, no matter how free we think it is.

Even with my new group of friends, witchcraft is following me. I hear the phone and Roger says, "Hey, want to come to a party?" "Oh, sure! This will be fun!" I get ready, and we meet. Everyone is there. The music is playing, and then boredom kicks in. Chrissy, one of my new friends, looks at me. "Hey, want to do some fun things?"

As I walk through the house, the party does not feel fun anymore. She looks at Roger and me, "Hey guys, have you ever done spells or things like that?" I know instantly what we are doing. I am used to this. Chrissy mentions that there is a spirit that needs a person. Oh. My heart is beating faster and faster. "I will do it!" "Why on earth are you doing this, Annetta?" I ask myself. Roger cares about me and is questioning it. "Are you sure? You don't have to do this." A fearful expression forms on my face, "No, I am ok. What do you want me to do?"

There is a table set up, and she points to the table. You must lie on this table and ask for this spirit to come into you. Roger looks concerned, "you don't have to do this." "I am ok." I say sheepishly as I form a fake smile. I lay down, and the familiar feeling comes to me back from my birthday party. The room turns dark. And as I repeat the words, the séance is complete.

My body feels strange. I don't feel right, and I feel out of control. As I get myself off the table, I need to catch my breath. I go outside and as I look at the trees, I hear a cackle and then fear tingles throughout my body. What have I done? I come back in and ask Roger to get me home, and as I am in the car, regret haunts me. And for now, I belong to the enemy. How far will I go? How much will I do to find the peace I am looking for?

Chapter 8
-Multiple Identities-

I am meeting all kinds of new people. My newest friends Valerie and Stephanie really like me too. These concerts and Emo friends are what I like. I can dress Emo and be whoever I want to be. Just not me. I don't like me. I am too boring without all these outfits. Without all these styles. If it's just me, they won't like me. I know I must keep trying. The drugs are helping, and my life is working. I don't always remember things. I show up late to school. I must drink before showing up to school, but that is the cost to be ok.

I can fit with the rage, punk posse, and skinhead. Whatever I need to be accepted. The mash pits and acid, and whatever drugs I need. But tonight, at this concert, I am not high yet. Everything feels fake. Everything feels lonely. Why am I even here? Looking around now, this strange guy splashes beer onto me. Cigarettes and drugs are passed around like candy. The ceiling has an opening that I can look through. The sky is black with a few stars shining through. There must be more to my life than this.

The feeling of not fitting in is stifling. I don't fit in with my new friends either. Until we all start talking about getting our heads shaved. Against my real desires, the next day I go to a salon. The sound of the buzzer is deafening. As my beautiful locks of hair fall to the ground, I am mortified. The hairdresser gasped as my hair was finished. I felt so ugly, but at least I could fit in with my new friends. The feelings of temporary joy disappear as quickly as they come in. Now I have no choice but to make the best of it.

Rumors are now spreading about another skinhead gang that wants to claim its territory in the downtown area. A threat is made, anyone wearing pink shoelaces with their boots will be made an example of if they go down this area on Friday at a certain time. We have pink shoelaces, so I tell my friends, "Let's do it!"

Valerie and Stephanie look at me and say, "It's crazy dangerous. They will literally beat us up or worse. The message is given to us so that we would stay clear of downtown that day and not test it out. I decide that if I must do it alone, I will. Friday comes, the day of the threat, and as I head downtown, I put my change in and find a quiet place to sit on the bus as my heart is pounding. Looking around with anticipation, I decide to get off the bus. Everything is in slow motion. I make sure to check out my surroundings with a cockiness that exudes stupidity.

As my feet are touching the ground, I look up and our eyes meet. It is the skinhead who made the threat. It was like an alarm went off in him, and he begins studying my boots. I walk past him, and I look back. I see that he is walking faster towards me. The adrenaline shoots through my body. I decide my best course of action is to run. As I look back again, he begins running faster towards me and yelling. He wants me to come back to him. I run faster than I ever have in my life. As I recklessly cross the street, I don't see any options.

I fearfully run into a Wendy's drive-through and beg a family to let me catch a ride to a bus stop since someone is chasing me. Surprisingly, they say yes. As we are driving away, I see the strange man who had been chasing me look around frantically, trying to see where I went. As the generous family drops me off at a bus stop, I know I barely missed death or a severe beating. Either way, I am thankful to get back home safely.

Chapter 9

-A Narrow Escape-

Stepping onto the bridge the darkness is calling me. I know I can do it. One time, it won't hurt anything. Pete, who I met just last week, is whispering in my ear, "You won't die. It's just rumors that say you will tangle in the weeds. You will swim safely to the side. Just do it." His voice gets louder. "Why are you scared, just jump! You are almost there." I begin to ascend the bridge again. The wind is getting stronger. The view is getting closer. Should I, do it? I think I can. Just one jump, just put one more foot up. As I look towards Pete a ghastly grin appears on him.

I feel like a jolt hits me as I look and see my friend Stephanie running up the road. Her screams wake me from the nightmare. "Annetta! Stop! What are you doing? Get off there! And you, get away from her! What are you doing?" Pete manages to barrage her with his obvious opinions. "She will not die; people jump from here all the time. She can simply swim to the side." Stephanie looks at him with disgust, "You are lying to her!" she blurts out.

I am now shielded by my friend Stephanie, and we slowly move away from the bridge. I feel so much shame as she looks at me. "Why would you do this? What were you thinking?" My mind begins racing. What if... what if I had jumped? The thought haunts me as we now silently make it back to the bus stop.

Chapter 10
-Spiraling Yet Hope Calling-

I open the car door and jump. My mom is yelling, "Annetta, don't you dare jump out of the car!" I hear her but it doesn't matter. Her words pierce deeply. She tells me how worried she is. She can tell I have been doing drugs, and I need help. She is pretending to take me out for fun and instead is planning on taking me to a rehab place. I am not going there. My heart is beating so fast as I run further and further from my mom. I can stop using drugs anytime, I tell myself. I don't need help. I find my way back home stewing in the anger I feel.

My cousin, Ronnie reaches out to my mom. He knows I am in trouble, and he wants to help. He tells my mom, "Hey if you give her a goal and let her earn the money, I think it would help her."

I hear a knock on the door and then the doorbell. My cousin Ronnie walks in with a loud shout and huge grin. "Annetta, so good to see you!" I peer at him with my dishevelled hair. He approaches me with joy and a leap in his step. I suspiciously look at him. "Want to hear something that will make you happy?

"Yes," I mutter under my breath. "What do you think about coming to live with me this summer? And earn money for something you have been wanting? What is something you have always wanted? What's your biggest dream? Anything? Just say it." I look up with trepidation. I softly mumble, "I have always wanted a motorcycle or scooter." Ronnie looks at me with great big eyes. "That's great!" as he turns excitedly towards my mom, and says, "How about it. How about we find her a scooter?" "Ok," my mom hesitantly says, and off we go to find my dream scooter.

As I find my way to his car, excitement fills the air. Could it be real? Could I have something I really want? We enter the store with anticipation, and only a few steps in, there it is, a beautiful red scooter. The scooter is highlighted to me. "There it is, Ronnie. That's the scooter I want." "Alright," he says with a big grin on his face.

We approach the salesman, and I softly say, "I want this scooter." As the salesman shares the price of over $1,500, I exhale with a wave of disappointment. I shout out, "How will I ever earn enough money for that?" Ronnie looks at me with stern and determined eyes, "If you want something bad enough, then you work hard for it and you can get things you want." With my heart leaping with delight, I say, "ok, I will do it." He prints out a picture of the scooter and says, "Focus on this, and when things get hard, realize this is your dream."

Plans are being made. I will go with Ronnie for the entire summer, starting a lawn mowing/edging business. Though thoughts of drugs and alcohol are plaguing me, the thought of this goal is helping me make it every day. There is happiness forming in my mind. Could life begin to get better for me? As I get closer to summer, the anticipation of this plan is mesmerizing. I focus on the picture of the scooter. Could this be real?

The day finally comes, and I get all my things packed, say my goodbyes, and off I go for an adventure. We arrive at his cozy home. I unpack and waste no time starting all the preparations. I get flyers made; he contacts friends in the area. Here we go. I follow in his footsteps. Day after day. Night after night. The work is paying off. The money is coming in.

The mornings are the hardest. I just want to sleep. I have no drugs, and I have no alcohol. I have no escape when my feelings come rushing in. I push through. We count the money daily. Finally, as summer is coming to an end, the final count is in. Can it be real? I have enough money. I did it! I can get the scooter. The air is lighter. My heart is so happy. I feel as if I can do anything. I can't wait to tell my mom.

Chapter 11

-Inconsequential? -

The drive home is quiet, heavy, and dull. Just minutes before, I feel on top of the world. I am so proud of myself in a good way. I pushed through this summer, and this wasn't supposed to happen. She was supposed to be happy for me. She was supposed to tell me how proud she was of me. She was supposed to, but it didn't happen.

Moments before, as I was gathering my things, I noticed my cousin was upset, along with my mom. He was raising his voice, "It will destroy her!" What will? I think to myself. As I move closer to their conversation, everything begins to slow down, almost like molasses. The words come from Ronnie: "Your mom is deciding that you can't have the scooter." My mom looks down at me through winced eyes, "Annetta, I am sorry, but you can't have the scooter." "What?" I say as I feel fire going through my veins, "but I earned it!"

My mind was numb, as everything I worked so hard for was slipping through my hands.

Why would she break my heart? While we are in the car, I sense Ronnie's disappointment in my mom. Even though he is fighting for me, it is useless. The gavel has been hit, the decision has been made. I will not be getting the scooter that I have focused on for all this summer, even though I had the money right now in my hand. A curse word slips out of my mouth, and my cousin reprimands me. I know, I say to myself, keep it all inside. I withdraw into a shell and won't speak the rest of the trip home, as a tear begins to fall down my face.

Chapter 12
-A Downward Tunnel with a Sight of Light-

The walls begin to build. What's the point of trying? I definitely deserve drugs now. All hope is gone. I have all this money now, for what? As I call my friends and vent my frustrations, only one thing makes sense. It's time to find friends and get high. I stuff my money into my sock. Not my smartest move. I pull it out to buy drugs, and half my money is missing. All the money I have earned is either gone or wasted away. I don't care as long as I can escape the reality of my life. Day after day, drugs and alcohol are all I want to do.

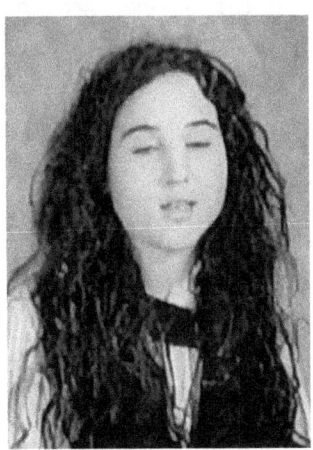

Drugged Out in 11th Grade

My heart is heavy, and it shows. I am so sad. Suicide again? Why not? Maybe the world would be better without me. Why am I here at this school? What's the point? Everyone hates me, and I hate everyone. I need more drugs or something. A voice jolts me out of my spiralling thoughts, "Hey, Annetta," says Ralph. "You look like you aren't doing well." "Nah," I say. Then he looks at me with his eyes of concern and care, "Hey, I used to struggle like you. There's a group of us. I am an alcoholic, and I found help. There's no shame in needing help. And I found my life is better now."

I look at him with narrow eyes, and hatred spews out of my mouth. "I am not an alcoholic; I am not like you. I can stop anytime. I don't have a problem. I am fine." But inside, I feel caught. Can someone see through me? I need to hide. But I am not able to. His eyes soften and he begins to say, "Ok, but a group of us are going to hang out like at a party tonight if you want to come hang out with us."

I scan him with my eyes, and curiosity overtakes me, "Can my friend come?" "Sure," he says with a big smile. I wonder if there will be drugs there, I think slyly. I feel a mix of excitement and nervousness as I prepare to go. As I tell Stephanie, always the skeptical one, she questions who they are. "They are from my school; I am sure it will be fine." Later that night, a large pickup with guys blaring music pulls up to us. Stephanie gives me a concerned look. "Are you sure about this?" I give her a devious grin and say, "Live a little!"

Our hair is blowing in the wind, as we are in the back of the pickup, and the air is sweet to breathe. I feel so alive. I don't know what is planned for the night, but I am sure it will be good. Suddenly, the truck stops on the side of the road near some houses. What is going on? Did I make a mistake? Oh, crap, what did I get us into? As the guys and Ralph step out of the car, they say, "We are at an alcoholics anonymous meeting." What the heck? My brother went to those when I was younger, so I was familiar with what they were. But he was a drug addict and alcoholic, not me!

Pride wells up in my body. With a crooked face and blistering voice, I yell, "How dare you? You are taking us to an AA meeting? How dare you? You tricked us? Why would you do this?" Cuss words come out, and I am hot all over. I jump out and say, "I am walking home." I yell and scream about what happened, not looking back. Ralph apologizes profusely as I begin to walk away. Stephanie is visibly upset too but tries to calm me down. What a miserably horrible day.

Chapter 13
-A Deadly Plunge-

How dare they trick us. I muster up more words about my disappointment. We don't have a problem. I don't have a problem, yet I can't seem to stay sober. I made it a while without drugs and alcohol this time, but the comments were getting more and more frequent. "Oh, Annetta, please get high again. You are so mad when you are sober."

Every time I hear my friends or family say it, the anger and fear begin to grow. I secretly hate how I feel when I am high or drunk, but it's the only way to survive. The fear is too deep. The pain is too much. Reality is too much to deal with.

But I can't keep going to it. I must try to stay sober. My phone begins to ring, and Valerie says in her sweetest voice, "Annetta, we are hanging out this weekend, you have to come over!" "Ok," I say shakily, "But I can't do any drugs." "Ok, but are you sure? You just seem so angry and upset all the time." I snap back, "No, I can't. I have to stay sober." Why won't she help me? Why is everyone against me? Don't they know my mom is making me see a counselor? I tell my counselor all the time that I can quit anytime, and I must prove that I am not an addict or alcoholic.

I look down, remembering I am at work, letting my boss know I will see her later. Little does she know what I have planned for tonight. Man, I love her. She is always there for me, but I think she knows. I think she knows that I come in here high a lot. Does she know that I haven't had any alcohol or drugs in like 2 or 3 months now? She must notice that I am angrier. I see the concern in her eyes. Well, whatever, I am not an addict. I know it. I will prove it to everyone, even tonight with my friends Valerie and Stephanie. I can say no. Or can I?

My shaky skateboard hits the ground. I love it. I feel so free. No one can tell me to stop. I just keep going. But why can't I breathe? Why am I feeling like I am suffocating with my emotions? Tears well up again. Why can't I be happy? As I come to my friend's tiny house, Valerie opens the door slowly and welcomes me in. She is genuinely excited to see me, but there's something about her eyes. What is she not telling me? There are more people here than I thought.

As the night goes on, Valerie pulls me aside, "We found someone who can give us some really good drugs. He is from the street, I have never met him, but my other friend knows him. It is supposed to be harder and better than all the other ones we have tried." Fear begins whispering in my ears. I feel my heart begin to pound. I look at Valerie with determined eyes, "I can't do it. I have been sober, and I don't want to do it," I say with a shaky voice.

Valerie looks at me with deep, trusting eyes. "Annetta, don't be scared. I will protect you. Nothing is going to happen to you. You can trust me." Trust? What's that? I think to myself. I haven't trusted anyone in a long time. I begin to cry as she holds me. She looks at me again, "I won't leave you; I will be with you the whole time. I promise nothing bad will happen to you." The doorbell rings. "They are here she says, giving me one last look and a ray of hope in her eyes that I will follow her down this path. With regret, I say, "One last time." Her eyes sparkle with delight, repeating my words back to me, "Ok, one last time."

The room begins to spin as we are all handed our drugs. Everyone takes it. I look at it incredulously. My hands begin to shake. "One last time", I keep repeating to myself. I make eye contact with Valerie. She smiles with the most comforting look she can muster. "Don't worry, I will be with you the whole time. Just have fun!" I look around and turn off every sense of logic, and I put the newfound drug in my mouth. Within 30 minutes, the room becomes jumbled. I can't think straight. Where is Valerie? She is my safe place. She begins laughing, and now I laugh.

Yet fear was now bigger. I see spiders, I shout, and look again. "Annetta, you are hallucinating! There are no spiders!" friends yell to me. What is real? I begin to question everything. I must get out of here. I close my eyes, and the visions begin to burn into my mind. There's no escape. Valerie promised she would be with me and protect me. Yet now I know it was an empty promise.

No one can help me. The morning comes. I am still seeing things. My friends look at me concerned. Are you still high? It's supposed to wear off. I am beginning to worry. The hours continue, and I am not coming down. Valerie and Stephanie look at me and say, "Maybe you should go home." Before I know it, two days pass. What was in that drug? What have I done? I head for my house, but I know I can't go home yet. What day is it? I find out it's going on for 3 days. I can't do this. What if I never come out of this? I heard of people like this. I can't stop seeing things.

As I am riding my skateboard, I am trying to escape from myself. This drug was different than any other I have tried. I may never think straight again.

I look up at the sky. It seems as if the world is slowing down. The words barely come off my tongue, "God, if you are real, help me." Suddenly, I remember Ralph. I remember he took us to a meeting downtown. I look around and to my surprise, I am sitting right where he took us the night of the party.

I look shiftily around, and there it is. The AA (alcoholics anonymous) building. I gather up what strength I have, pick up my skateboard, and make my way up the hill through heavy fog and knock on the door. I place my shaky hands on the doorknob, open the door, and walk in.

Chapter 14
-A New Beginning-

Smoke fills the room. Old men and women are sitting around. One of their eyes catch mine. With big, beaming eyes, I hear, "Welcome." The next woman comes to me, and all I can muster in a small, trembling voice is, "I need help." I feel an embrace. My body begins to calm. A friendly voice speaks out, "Have a seat and just listen." Coffee is offered, and though I feel fear, there's something I've never felt. Is that hope?

If I could stay all night, I would. I feel so safe here. No one is judging me. I tell them that one of my friends drove me here, and that's why I knew where they were. The atmosphere is intoxicating in a good way. The shaking has to stop, right? I ask if I will ever get rid of the high. No one really knows but God. And I am praying for it to stop. I feel life, yet fear. Will I ever be the same again?

One of the women is concerned for me. With worried eyes asks, "Where are you going? How are you getting home?" As I relay my predicament, she says she will give me a ride home. I don't know these people. I don't know her, but I feel safe. I feel they are trustworthy. I make the descent down the hill, and we drive. She questions what I am doing at this age, doing drugs and drinking. I look blankly and say, "I don't know." I am the youngest one there and feel like a child to them. I am a child, actually still a teenager. As she drops me off, her words ring in my ears. "Keep coming back ".

As I sneak into my home, I am relieved to get into my bed. The next day, though still shaky, my head is beginning to clear. I keep finding AA meetings and realize I am an alcoholic and addict. Though everything is still blurry, one thing is clear: I must keep coming back. They understand me and help me without expecting anything in return. God has shown me he is real. He is getting me help, and the drugs are gradually leaving my body.

I look it up; there is a meeting down the road from my house. I don't care anymore. I need help. I am willing to do whatever it takes to stop using it. I just want freedom. As I walk down the road, I find the building, and with every ounce of courage I can find, I walk in.

The men and women are so friendly. "Welcome, welcome, welcome," they all say as hands are put in front of me. "Nice to meet you, a tall, friendly older man says. The room is so big. When I find my seat, there are dozens and dozens of people. One person raises their hand. "Hello, I am Ricky, and I am an alcoholic." The crowd answers back, "Hello, Ricky, welcome." The environment is rich with laughter and wit. My legs keep moving. I am shaking and can't stop. I am so embarrassed, so exposed. I look up, and tears begin to pool in my eyes. I can't hide this. I can't hide who I have become.

I listen intently and see the steps on the wall. The lines are moving, but I manage to read them. Admit you are powerless and need help from a higher power. Higher power? What? Like God? Well, that's what got me to this meeting. Yes, I need help. As my thoughts are racing through my head, I am greeted by so many people repeatedly, sharing how happy they are to see me there.

The warmth I feel makes me want to keep coming back. One lady says, "The shaking will stop, you are just detoxing." As I leave the building and head back home, I think this is it. This is where I can get better. It's like a hospital for the hurting, and I am definitely hurting.

Chapter 15

-A Long Road Ahead-

Day after day, attending these meetings, the shaking has stopped. My mind is coming back. I am no longer high. I can breathe. Every day, I am asking God to keep me sober. I admit I am powerless. I must tell my family and counsellor, and even my boss what is happening. Everyone is happy for me except for my family. They don't think I am fun anymore, though it hurts, I don't care. I need this. I finally feel I can get help.

One day, I realize I need a sponsor. Hey, I think to myself, I have prayed before, and things happened. I ask God to show me who should be my sponsor. As I walk into the meeting, I look over to the right side. Sitting in a chair, it's like a light is shining on her. Her voice was dripping with peace. That's her! I want what she has.

After the meeting, I approach her. Sheepishly, I look at her and whisper, "Will you be my sponsor?" She says her name is Noreen, and with a look of intensity I have never seen, says, "Are you willing to work the program and do everything I ask you to do?" Ever so energetically, I say, "Yes! I will do it." "Ok, she says, let me think about it and I will get back to you." I am hearing what some people think God is like. All I know is that I can't be sober without him. I am so desperate.

On my way to work, I see the beauty of the hills, and I get down and pray to God. I didn't know it, but Noreen was driving by and sees me. Every day, I am praying and asking God to help me. Finally, Noreen finds me at a meeting, "I am willing to sponsor you, but it will take work." I look at her and with puppy dog eyes, and say, "Yes, and thank you!" We begin working the AA steps, and I am willing to do whatever she asks.

One day, during step 4, where we confess all our sins, she looks at me and with complete seriousness says, "Annetta, the only thing that will help you get rid of this fear is Jesus."

I look at her with confused eyes. "Really?" Deep inside, I realize I heard this name before. I heard it at church when my mom would drag me as a little kid, holding onto my coat, dragging me across the parking lot. That can't be it. That can't be who she's talking about. That can't be where she gets her peace. I don't know who this Jesus is, but I know that when I went to that church, all I felt was bad. I felt bad about myself. I felt condemned.

I look up and question her. I am angry. I am upset, yet I had nothing else. "I will think about it," I say with a hint of rebellion. I get home and soon find a letter from one of my old druggie buddies. Annetta, I have found God. I have found Jesus and wanted to tell you about it. It is long. It is genuine.

She says I need to surrender my life to Jesus. She is telling me what Noreen says. Everywhere I go, it's on my mind. This Jesus guy. Is this who I have been searching for? I still am praying, God, is this you? Is this who you are?

Chapter 16

-An Unlikely Encounter-

I get up on a morning just like any other morning. I have to get to High School and then my part-time job. Here I am sitting on the bus, minding my own business. I look up. This lady gets on the bus and looks so strange. She smiles at me. Her long flowing blond hair and white dress stand out to me. She approaches me, "Hey, how are you doing? Have you heard about Jesus?" She begins sharing about him. I look at her with disbelief. Not another one. Why is it everywhere I go that his name is coming up? Jesus, this Jesus that.

"Are you considering Jesus?" I look at her with irritation. Why don't people just leave me alone? I look at her and say, "I don't know. I haven't decided yet." I nervously look at the full bus. Everyone is looking down at other things. It's like no one sees her. (This is before everyone has phones.) It's like she is invisible. With bated breath, I say goodbye, and she encourages me to consider the bible and Jesus.

It feels as if there is a tug of war. I want freedom and I want God, but I am scared. Is Jesus the answer? I don't know. It's scary. What if it's not true? What if I make the wrong choice? After all, I followed Satan. I tried New Age. I tried Buddhism. I tried so many things. Is this the right one? The wrestling was getting harder and harder. What do I do? God, is this you? Is this the real God? I didn't want anything but the real God.

I get on the bus, and there she is again. I think she must be an angel. Again, she's wearing a white dress and blond hair. She approaches me and asks me if I have decided what I want to do. She begins to share more about the bible with me. In confusion, I say, "I don't know. It's all so much." She patiently answers me. "Just think about it." Again, I feel like there is a tug of war for me. I get off the bus. Maybe this is for real. It's like everywhere I go, Jesus is coming up. I am told that when I am ready, I can pray by myself or with someone else.

Finally, I make it to another AA meeting. The meeting ends. I look up outside. I need to know who God is. I whisper quietly, "I can't keep fighting you, Jesus. I asked you who you were, and your name keeps coming up." It feels like God keeps bringing people into my path. I feel so foolish talking out loud, and yet it feels natural. "Ok. You win." As I look up into the beautiful night sky, I get on my knees slowly. I begin the prayer from my heart.

I now know what I need to do. I boldly say, "Jesus, I ask you to forgive me for everything I have ever done. I confess that you are the Son of God. You died on the cross, and you rose three days later from the grave. I believe you are real, and I ask that you now come to live in my heart." The words are finished, and as I look up, I see something. The clouds are parting. I know something happened. I did it. I accepted Jesus as my Lord and Savior. I receive him with everything inside of me.

This is what I have been searching for. This is the true God. The God of the bible is the one I have needed and wanted, and the only one that can forgive me and take away all my fear. I don't feel it quite yet, but I know there is something happening.

I must tell Noreen. I have to tell others. I have finally said Yes! I call Noreen and she meets with me. I let her know, and I said Yes! She screeches with delight! She looks straight into my eyes and, in all seriousness, says, "Now you are forever with him! I am so excited for you, Annetta!" I do feel different. Is that peace I feel? I tell my family, though they aren't as excited as I hoped they would be. The party girl is now gone.

Days pass, and I must get on the bus to head to work after school. I sit down and I see her. She comes and sits down, and I look at her with bold eyes and say, "I decided to say yes. I have accepted Jesus." Her eyes are filled with delight, "I am so happy for you! If you want, you can have this bible." She begins telling me all the things to study. In a mom tone, she says, "Make sure you read your bible and pray daily." Her eyes light up. Her stop is up, and as she walks away, she waves at me. Little did I know I would never see her again...

Chapter 17
-Steps Taken, Steps Lost-

Life is going fast. I feel better. It is almost as if a huge weight has been lifted. People are talking. They say I look different. What has happened? Though for months now I have been separated from my druggie friends, I muster up the courage to invite Stephanie to a worship event. The music is sweet. The drums beat fast, and the lyrics lift my heart. He has given me a second chance. Can Stephanie feel it? Does she know that God is real? She must see the difference.

Her eyes look through me with hurt and yet wonder. I wait for the night to end and tell her. I turn to her and, with a wide-eyed expression, say, "I have changed. I found out God is real. He has given me a new chance, and you can have it too." Her eyes glaze over. I know she hears me, but she isn't ready. I know I must let her go, but my heart hurts. Why can't my friends come with me? I still feel self-conscious knowing I left. If she wants this, I can only tell her. It's up to her.

I have to get healing from my past. Noreen tells me I must make amends, "If I did anything wrong, I need to make it right. This is the way to get free." I know, though my hands are trembling, it's the right thing to do. The phone rings, and with bated breath, I wait for Rita to answer the phone. The shock as she hears my voice is evident. I try to muster up the courage to face the girls who hurt me and who I hurt just a few years ago. "Annetta, why are you calling?" What do you want?" The snarkiness lingers. "I wanted you to know I forgive you. I forgive you for everything. And I want to ask you to forgive me."

The awkward silence is deafening. Her sister Tori grabs the phone. I hear Rita laughing in utter disbelief that I would have the nerve to call them. The ending of our friendship was abrupt years ago. They still hate me. Many things happened, including making out with their friend's brother and ignoring them after their witch friend came to my house. Tori and Rita hated me for it. I explain that I am trying to make things right and am sober now. Before the last word is finished, I hear the click of the phone.

Everything around me is spinning. How many people do I need to talk to? Besides that, my family seems stressed. What is happening? My grandma is sick. It seems like everyone is included in helping my grandma, except me. I want to know what's happening. I love her so much. Memories flood my mind. I am a young child sitting on one of her many rocking chairs. "Come and get some lemonade, Annetta!" she says with a cheerful look. I bring the drink to the back porch. You can't hear a car, plane, or anything, except the sounds of nature. A grasshopper jumps close to the ground.

A bird is chirping with happy songs. The wind is blowing gently against the screen door. The air is crisp. It is fresh. It's almost as if I have no trouble in my life. I feel something. What is it? It feels like peace. Suddenly, my mind brings me back to reality. Grandma. The one that is always so secure. The one place that I can find comfort and feel so safe. What? Is she dying? The thoughts fill my mind.

I cannot bear the thought of losing her. She is so strong. She is so funny. She loves God. She knows me and still always welcomes me back. Please, God, don't tell me she's gone. Please say she will be ok. I have just given my life to you. Please do not take away my grandma.

I look down. I know it has been weeks since she got sick. What is that? My mind tries to comprehend what I am reading. A white piece of paper with only two words. Two words that will change my life forever. Grandma died....

Chapter 18
-Look Up-

Pain pierces my heart. It's deep. I can't breathe. I can't see clearly. I muster out one sound. The pain makes its way down my throat. It continues to travel. It goes deeper. It continues down a dark path. The ending is not in sight. My voice shakes. The words fall flat. God help me. The tears form in my eyes; they're like a waterfall. I see her face again. I hear her voice. I remember like it's yesterday. Another memory pops up. I hear her voice as a kid. She strongly, yet sweetly calms me as she says, "Annetta, you have nothing to be afraid of," as I climb into her bed, shaking. "What if someone comes in here and hurts us?" Her calming voice steadies me.

Just days before, I come to her house, and with a sweet grin, she says, "There's something in there for you." I know what it is. Every time I come to her ranch, she hides a present.

I run into the living room, and everyone watches. I lift the top off the ottoman. A present! A toy! Excitement fills my heart along with a sense of love. I shout out, "Thank you, Grandma!" Memories flood my mind. And yet here I am. Reality hits me. I will never see her again.

How much grief can I take? Now I visit my uncle, and his body looks like a skeleton. His face is withering. He wasn't the uncle I remember. The building is cold, lifeless, and uncomfortable. I whisper to God, if I need to share something, please make a way. Everyone leaves, and it's just me and him. I muster the strength to talk to him with my heart racing. My words almost seem dull, yet poignant. "Do you know the only hope there is? Do you know?" as I point to my bible. He nods and says, "Yes, I believe, Annetta", he whispers in a tired, strenuous way. I know his time will come soon. I just must make sure he knows...the truth. I want him to know the truth. Now I know I will see my uncle again.

My mind goes back to when I was seeing my counselor several months ago. Before everything started happening with my grandma and Uncle, I remember going every week. I visit her in this building behind me. She questions me, "Can you really stop using drugs and alcohol anytime?" Defensiveness rises in me. "Yes, I can. I am not an addict or alcoholic." I say vehemently. Her patience is steady. She doesn't break. But there's something different about her. She comes limping in with her oxygen tank. She pours out to me. How does she do it? I don't care; my selfish heart says, consumed with my own life. She gently encourages me and pays no attention to her struggles just to help me.

I come back different this week; I admit to her that I am an alcoholic and addict. The words come off my tongue gently this time. I finally admit it. I am getting help. I am sober now. Really sober. I found God. He is helping me. Her words go deep: "I am proud of you, Annetta." Her mothering voice comforts me. Our bond is deep.

Reality hits hard now. I just saw her weeks ago. How could she leave? How could she die? How could all of them die? A painful dart hits again. This cry goes deep. It goes 3 people deep.

Chapter 19

-This New Life-

I pause. I look back. Just a few months ago, I said yes to Jesus. Noreen calls. "Annetta, would you like to get baptized? "We are planning on going out to the lake this weekend." I don't know what to expect. Fear still has a grip on me. I sheepishly agree. The day comes. Our whole small bible group comes. There's another girl new to the group who will get baptized today too. The car ride is bumpy, awkward, and exciting at the same time. When we get out of the car, the path is muddy. I make my way through the trees. One hits me as I follow behind the others. "Where are we going?" I yell out. Another friend says, "You will see Noreen's husband up ahead."

I push the branches from my head. We walk for what feels like forever. The smell of the dirt and fragrance of flowers is all around me. Finally, I push back the last branch, and an open lake is found. The still pond water is inviting, welcoming, yet scary. I know this is my last step in confessing that I am now following Jesus. Why am I hesitant, though? Will this be real? The first girl goes in. He proclaims her baptism with all the zeal as John the Baptist. He resembles John the Baptist, with a large beard and flowing hair. His conviction is strong. He knows what he believes is true. Next, he calls my name.

I slowly enter the water. The mucky, still water. I don't know what is lurking underneath, but bravery comes to me every step I take. I grab his hand awkwardly, yet I have the determination to finish what I have started. In a booming voice, he asks me, "Annetta, do you confess Jesus as your Savior? And do you believe he died on the cross and rose three days later?"

The words echo through me, "Do you make a public profession to follow him (Jesus) all your life?" I answer with a gentle breath, "Yes, I do."

Jeff gently leads me, with confidence in his voice, "Annetta, I baptize you in the name of the Father, the Son, and the Holy Spirit." As I rise from the water, I feel it, the excitement. I am told my old man is gone; the new man is now alive. I don't quite understand, but I believe this is a fresh start. A new beginning. Though doubt is still whispering, is this the only way? I know deep in my heart it is. I am in. I am in a new family, and I am a new person.

Chapter 20
-The Spoils-

I put my black gown on. My hair must be just right. My mom helps me with my cap. It's happening. It's really happening. Flashbacks of the last year hit me. All I have been through, and I am still graduating? How? How is it possible? I haven't had a drink of alcohol or drugs in over a year. My mind is racing. What if I fall? Who is going to be there watching?

The hours go by like minutes. We arrive. The anticipation is beyond me. My hands are shaking. My eyes are watering. My heart feels as if it will explode. I look up. All my family is here. Joy fills the atmosphere.

My new friends from AA are here. My sponsor with her family is here. I have never known such joy. Such love. As I am called up into line, I hear my name, and everything is in slow motion. As I shake hands and get my diploma, my eyes scan the audience.

There is clapping, there are shouts, as if a symphony is behind me. Happiness and joy overwhelm me. I have worked hard and by God's grace, I throw my cap in the air after I hear the words I have been waiting for. Congratulations Graduates!!!

I sense it. I sense the freedom that is for me. Something is awakened in me. There is joy in my life. Desires I never thought possible. Months pass, and I know God has given me a new life. After seeing the Nutcracker, I had to dance. It was as if a gift within me was coming to the surface. I knew this was it. I put my hand on the door, and as I pull it open, it's as if a new world opens to me.

Girls and boys dressed in their parts. As my mouth opens, embarrassment shades my face. "I am here to dance." "Have you danced before?" the owner asks curiously. "No, not really", I say timidly. "That's ok, you can start with our beginner class if you don't mind dancing with five-year-olds." I agree and I work harder than I ever have before.

My first performance is here. All the moments. All the dedication, all the fear of stepping out, and it's here. I feel alive as I enter the dance floor. My part is a solo. I hear the applause. My family and friends are cheering as they did at graduation. Could this be real? Could good things come into my life? I never believed I could be happy. Maybe my life could be better.

Chapter 21
-Things Given, Things Taken-

He threw the keys into the air. I catch them with disbelief that he would do such a thing. Me? I don't even know you that well, I think to myself. My friend Kathy looked at me and said, "Yes, he is giving you, his car!" I am not used to this. The car I had been given was totaled by the drunk driver who hit it in my parents' driveway. I prayed for a new car, but I was still used to riding the bus everywhere. God is showing me how real he is in my life every day; it seems. Days pass, months pass, and I am seeing God's goodness everywhere I go.

I am sharing how much God loves others. I am thriving in my home church, and now I have discovered a new brick-and-mortar church, but I still don't know how to take care of my belongings, especially my new car.

I am driving to work, to my same job, and as I look, the car begins to slow down. The engine begins with a strange choking noise. Oh no! I begin to slow down. The car shakes until it reaches a full stop. I turn the car to the side of the highway. I don't have a phone; I can't tell my boss I am running late. What do I do? My brain returns to what it always did before. I can hitchhike. I used to do it all the time. I temporarily lose my way as I stick my thumb out. I am sure I will be fine, right?

Chapter 22

-Fight, Flight, Run-

Minutes pass, and the walking is getting too tiring. His car comes creaking up, as his window goes down, an older dishevelled man appears. His friendly voice beckons me closer. "Hey, Miss, do you need a ride?" An uneasiness rises inside of me. I begin to look down. He senses it. "He bellows out. You probably have a long walk. You can trust me! I can give you a ride to where you need to go." Common sense and desperation are pulling me in opposite directions. Do I go? Do I keep walking and lose my job for being late yet again?

"Ok," I say warily, opening the back door. I have enough sense to be in the back seat instead of the front. He jovially asks about my life, "Where are you going and working?" I try to pretend to be interested, but each turn, fear is getting bigger and bigger. God, what have I done? I know better. Please help me. He bemoans having to make another stop before he takes me to my destination. The shakiness in his voice causes me to question his intentions.

Annetta, get out of the car. The voice I hear is getting louder and louder in my head. He is taking a few minutes at the store we stop at. I can easily get out. He comes back from the store to the car with a jump in his step. He seems awfully excited. I should have left when I had the chance. My heart begins to skip a beat after we pull out of the store and begin the drive yet again, and he pulls out a pornographic magazine. "You like this?" he asks in a perverted, intense look. I yell, "No! and before I can think, I unlock the door and jump out of the car. As I am mid-air, I hear him yelling, "You can't do that!"

My body tumbles to the ground, and I quickly get up. I see and hear strangers yelling out of the car, "Are you ok?" My hands and voice shaking, I manage a feeble "I'm ok," but really, I am not ok. I manage to get to the bus stop and decide I cannot do that again. I make my way to work and explain to my boss my harrowing escape.

Chapter 23
-Cult? -

Though bad things still happen, I still am seeking God. After all, he was the one telling me not to get in that car. I have so many new amazing friends now. God is giving me new ones to replace the old ones. I love meeting new people. I keep hearing about speaking in tongues. Is it real? I want to try it, but I don't know exactly how. At this conference, I am sure everyone will be amazing. Though Shelly seems different than the others. We connect so much that she invites me to her church after the conference.

I find the address and enter the building. I shyly enter and let them know, "I am friends with Shelly, and she said to come there." I am welcomed warmly by so many kind people. The first person I meet looks at me with a big smile and says, "Hi, my name is Riana." We begin talking. Days turn into weeks. I am loving this new church. Riana is so friendly. She invites me to another church. "You are going to love my other church! But it's a little bit of a drive." "It's ok," I say, "I want to go." As we drive through the country roads, it is eerily quiet. When we enter the home, I am greeted by Mama Cathy. "How nice to meet you," she says with a creepy smile. The air is filled with the aroma of buttery biscuits. I look at the table, and there is a basket full of homemade goodies. "Would you like one, dear?" I say, "yes," sensing a nurturing mother figure. She offers another biscuit after I gobble down the first one. I ignore the hesitancy and lack of peace in my heart. I am sure these are nice people. I know it's just me feeling this, I think while trying to mask my trepidation.

We head to church, and I notice everyone is wearing skirts. I stand out. I feel embarrassed as I am wearing pants. I don't fit here. Their worship is simple. It's nice. Everything is nice, but maybe a little too nice.

Riana looks at me. "What do you think?" "It's nice," I say. "Is it ok that I don't wear dresses?" "Sure, it's fine. They don't care. There is no pressure. I want you to stay and meet everyone, and later tonight we will do some coon hunting. It's so much fun!" Coon hunting? I guess that could be fun, but a little weird, I think to myself. The whole day and night are so fun. But I can't shake this feeling. There's no peace. But maybe again, it's just me.

Riana gives me a ride back to my house. As I think about it, I try to convince myself that this church might be for me. Next week, Riana invites me to come out again. Now that I keep coming, maybe the skirts aren't so bad. They talk in these sermons about it. And I want to fit in. Perhaps I can sell all my pants and just wear skirts. Why do Noreen and Jeff have to keep telling me to stop going? Yes, I told them I want to get rid of all my pants and become a member of this church, but what's the harm? They keep telling me it's a cult. It's not a cult! They just don't understand it. Maybe Noreen and Jeff need to relax.

Sunday is here again. I have my skirt on, and I think I will get baptized here. They said to become a part of their church, you need to get baptized with them. Yes! I can do it. I was already baptized, but it's ok. Riana seems so happy with me since I have decided only to wear skirts. I am finally coming around. And now to get baptized? So amazing!

I declare it again. I get the microphone and tell them I know Jesus is real now. I declare it. I know baptism is here. I do it. They baptize me. I feel I am new again. I am fully immersed. This is my home now. But why do I keep getting told I am in a cult? Do I have to wear skirts? Is it only a small group? Maybe this church will be the only one going to heaven? Why can't anyone understand? I feel almost numb.

Noreen and Jeff must be praying. They heard I sold all my pants and am actively involved in this church. It's like, why aren't they supporting me?

But why do I feel this way? The peace is not here. I am trying. I am trying so hard. Is this you, God? Why doesn't this feel right? My eyes close, my brain remembers what it felt like before. Suddenly, it's as if I see a cliff. I am laughing my way down to the cliff. I must get out of this. I must. It's like when I jumped out of the car. They aren't as bad, but something is saying, "Get out!!!!" I jump, and now it's time to tell them.

I find Riana, I can't keep going here. I don't feel this is right for me. "Why?" she asks with bewilderment in her voice. "You know that if you leave this church, you will go to hell, right? Fear grips me. Another woman on the phone, whom I tell I left the church, answers back, with the creepiest voice I have heard, "I am afraid that you are going to go to hell now." I muster all the courage I have and say, "No, I won't," and hang up. Thank God I got out. Now time to get back to what God has for me.

Chapter 24
-The Start of Something New-

But I don't want to go. God is asking me again. One of my roommates at this new place I am in just got back. She has changed for the better. She is confident, with a new light in her eyes. But if God is asking me to go, "What if I die? What if I must get on a plane again? I hate planes. They are scary. I don't want to. I just can't do it."

Now here I am at this amazing church service. The worship is sweet. I love feeling God's peace and his presence. But wait, what am I feeling? I have learned what God's voice sounds like. It's like everywhere I go, every magazine talks about going on mission trips.

My heart beats fast, I look up, and I almost hear something profound in my heart. "Are you going to follow me or not?" I have already decided to follow Jesus. So yes, I will follow. How could I not? I have nowhere else to go. I know what God is asking me. Will I go on a mission trip by myself? God is asking me to go, and it is a firm ask with a lot of love. "Ok, okay I say as if I am a small child being reprimanded." I will go.

The pages are heavy and weighty. The magazine I saw it in. Where was the outreach I saw? There it is, almost coming off the page. I know this is it. I pick up the phone and, with trepidation in my voice, I ask the girl on the phone about their outreach to Venezuela. Excitement enters my heart. I know I am being obedient, but fear is trying to choke my life out. I must do this. I want to be close to Jesus, and this is what he is asking me to do.

If God wants me to do this, he needs to provide the money. My current boyfriend, Ricky, calls me, "Yes, they want to meet with you. The church I attend is so sweet. The worship is intimate. It is real, and it is nothing like the cult I went to. The pastor looks at me with genuine eyes, "I will pray about it, Annetta."

If this is from God, he will make it happen. I have already seen him answer prayers for me. My phone rings. In anticipation, I answer. The pastor sounds happy, hopeful as he says, "Yes, we decided to cover your whole trip." "What? Oh my gosh, thank you so much! I can hardly believe it! I am going on my first mission trip! I can't breathe. I am so excited, yet how is my family going to respond? They are already skeptical of my newfound faith.

It's been weeks since I found out I am going to Venezuela. My family looks at me with wide, confused eyes as almost everyone cries out, "What, why? On Christmas day?" Everyone looks at me with shocked faces. "Annetta, this is crazy! You are leaving on Christmas Day? Out of all days! And you don't know anyone? Are you going to be ok?" This does not seem right, they tell me, but with confidence, I tell them God has told me to go.

I need to obey him and do what he says to do; I will be fine." Exasperated, they have no choice but to say goodbye. My Mom looks at me with worry and fear in her eyes, "I hope you know what you are doing." "I do, and I have to do this."

As she drops me off at the airport, I feel the love and tension she feels. I am her baby. She is bringing me here, but I can tell her heart is heavy. The buzzing of cars around me is deafening. The planes are zooming all around. Fear is knocking, but faith is louder. "Bye, Mom, I love you.

I feel a mixture of fear and peace. God, help me. Only you can. The plane is scary, but you are with me, Jesus. Yes, we landed. I made the first trip. I step out of the plane, and there's the group, the mission group leader. Dizziness makes me hardly able to breathe. I am led quickly. I look around, and another young girl is there too. I am not alone.

The room is small. We all must sleep here. The meeting begins, and first thing in the morning, we will head to Venezuela. I look around, new faces all around me. Anxiety is creeping up. I don't know these people, yet I must travel across the world? What have I gotten myself into?

Morning comes, all ready. We are going on an adventure. I know God is with me. I pray a desperate prayer. God, please help me. Please be with me as I go on the plane to Venezuela. Help me. I feel his closeness. He loves me. He is so proud of me. As I look up, it's as if I can sense Jesus covering me and helping me. We board our first flight.

Not too bad. We board the second plane. It feels shaky. It's small. God, please let us land safely. As we finally touch down, the passengers begin to clap. Cheers are heard everywhere. Strange to clap, but I was clapped too. Relief hit me. I survived the tiny plane ride. As we exit, we are surrounded by the most beautiful mountains. The air is different, almost as thick as a blanket. A musty smell fills my nose, and I am filled with wonder. The bigness of this place overwhelms me.

I know you called me here, but it is so difficult. The days begin blurring together. What have I done? Why am I here? I feel so alone—none of the other guys and girls like me. I think. I feel so rejected. Why did I come here again? God, please don't leave me like this. I have obeyed you. I cry and cry, leaders look at me, "You are accepted. You are loved, so many people would give anything to be here like you." "I know, I just am struggling," I say with anxiety creeping up yet again.

I get on the bus. No one sits with me. It's ok, I tell myself, trying to stop the lies from Satan himself. As we reach this new village, the leader, Scott, preaches with a boldness I have never heard. "If you want prayer, we will go out to you." I see her. She must be six or seven years old. Awkwardly, I ask her if she wants prayer.

Boldness hits me. "Do you want to ask Jesus into your heart and ask for forgiveness? Her eyes widen, "Yes, I do." I lead her in a heartfelt prayer. She follows my words with expectancy. Afterwards, she finishes, and a joyful smile flashes on her face. "Thank you so much." She gives me a coin to thank me and rushes off.

Our group meets. "Did anyone have anything happen? Little things here and there. Not a lot happened. I raise my hand, "I led a little girl to Jesus; I say with a timid voice. "That's wonderful, Annetta!" I realize, as hard as this has been, maybe that's why I came all the way here. I was meant to lead this little girl to Jesus. God must love her a lot to bring somebody from America to tell her about himself. I whisper to Jesus, "Thank you," and a special peace fills my fear-filled heart.

It has been almost 2 weeks since we arrived here. These last few days, I am going to make it count. I look out at the house, and gratitude fills my heart. I am thankful, though tired. We decide to go out one more time to a restaurant. Christy, a long-term missionary there, knows all the places to eat. "This one is safe. We can eat here with no issues."

Owww. What is wrong with my stomach? I can't stop, oh my gosh, I have to throw up. The world is spinning. As I look up in our dorm room, I see everyone leaning out of bed. Throwing up and moaning. "Oh no. We must leave tomorrow morning, and it looks like they got sick from the restaurant," says one of the leaders.

The morning is here, and we all still feel awful. The plane ride is horrible. My stomach hurts so bad. Why did I have to eat there? Ughhhhh. Finally, I never thought the plane would land.

My mom sees me and looks at me frantically. Her eyes narrow with concern. "Why did I let you go?" I am sick, Mom, from what I ate. We'll get to the doctor as soon as possible. At the doctor's office, the words slowly come out of his mouth, "Sorry, it looks like you have parasites. Take this medicine, and it should resolve the issue. I feel horrible, but I obeyed God and should be done with missions now, and I got to lead a little girl to Jesus.

Chapter 25

-Almost Stopped-

I'm done, right? Right God? Youth With a Mission is coming up everywhere I go now. I already went to Venezuela. Wasn't that enough? I have a good life here. I have a job. I have Ricky, I have friends, I have dance, and I am sharing you with others, Jesus. My thoughts are swirling. For now, I can tell others about Jesus at this bus stop. I look around, he will do. His face is angry. Sad, almost lost. He needs to hear about Jesus.

My heart is beating fast as I approach him. He is alone and wearing a dark colored jacket. As I get closer, I feel something unusual. I feel fear and hesitation. I can sense God is telling me no, not him. I argue, "But God, he needs to hear the gospel."

As I open my mouth and begin sharing the good news, a creepy grin appears on his face. Almost abruptly, he says, "I must catch another bus at a different bus stop. You can continue telling me while we walk. I look down, I hear and sense almost a scream, "Do Not Go with Him. Stop! This is not okay!" In my stupidity, I think I know better than God. I push my sense aside.

With each step, I feel more fear. I keep my distance as I am sharing with him. He looks at me, pretending to be interested. We keep walking. I feel myself going behind him. "We are almost there. Why do you keep staying away? It's ok." The path gets darker.

We come to a sidewalk. I get quiet. There is no one around. I see streetlights and almost wish there were more of them. I see the lone bus stop up ahead. There is no one there. I realize I am in trouble. We make it to the stop. I feel him come from behind me. "Almost a whisper, I have a knife, and I am going to kill you." I whisper, "Jesus, help me", as he pushes me down, and I make a pitiful scream. I know this is it.

I look up. Why is he running? He won't look back. He has seen something. No one is here. At least no one that I can see. I know something or someone saved me. I know God saved me. With trembling hands, I find a gas station and call the police. I describe what just happened. I should not be alive. I know God helped me by sending an angel or something to save me. I will listen next time.

Chapter 26
-Forgiveness-

"Why would you do that?" my brother looked at me incredulously. "He doesn't deserve forgiveness." I know, but I chose to forgive him. Though traumatized by what happened just days ago, I knew I had to forgive him. Advice was pouring in. Everyone is worried about me. Friends are asking if I should still go to YWAM. I have to. I know what God is saying. But my friends all say the same thing. "Are you sure you should go? You are still so broken. The attack just happened a couple of months ago."

Everywhere I go, there he is in my mind. I must go out and meet some friends. My heart begins to race. Is that him? The guy who attacked me? No, just looked like him. I can't function; I can't breathe. It's hard to sleep at night. Forgiveness is never easy. It's hard when someone hurts you to release them. But that is what I must do.

During worship, I hear another message about forgiveness. I know I have forgiven this random guy, but is there more? Yes. Memories start flooding in. The one who abused me. Him? He asked for my forgiveness, but did I forgive him? I feel God reminding me again. Look at what I did for you. I have forgiven you for everything. Sometimes you don't have to feel it to forgive. I decide to forgive the family member, too. Now I am choosing to forgive my dad. Those memories flood in. He abused my friends, actually my closest friends, Stephanie and Valerie, who were also in high school.

I did not even know when it happened. Stephanie told me on a phone call a few years ago. The memory still triggered me with rage. My mind brings me back to the moment when she shares details of what happened. All I can manage to say is, "I am so sorry." My words hit the ground as monotone as a computer agent. The phone itself drops as if falling into a pit of nothingness. Anger begins to fill my betrayed heart. Why did he do it? Why would he? I suddenly am shot back into the church event. It is wrong, it's not fair.

He has not even apologized. He doesn't deserve my forgiveness. Yet, as if I hear a whisper, forgive him." Jesus hung on the cross, looking at those who betrayed him. Hurt him. What did he say? He said, "Father, forgive them for they know not what they are doing." He didn't say, "Nah, y'all are too much. Too many sins. Too gross. Too mean. Too much. He forgives. "If you do not forgive others, God will not forgive you." It seems harsh. I have been through so much. God, I cry out, God, I want to be close to you. I need help or a desire to forgive them.

Help me to forgive them. I release a little. My hand opens a little bit—I have a willingness to forgive. And little by little, as my heart opens, the war inside gets a little quieter.

Chapter 27
-Say Hello, Say Goodbye-

As I drive off, there they are. There are my best friends I am leaving behind. They threw me a farewell party last night and prayed over me. Now, as my mom and I are driving off to YWAM, I turn my head somberly, and I see them waving. I cry looking back and realizing I may never see them again. The reality of this adventure hits me. My mom, though nervous, still drives me. I am grateful.

She knows that God is with me and helps me, and she has seen me get sober. She knows this is real. The long drive there, I pray. I am scared and yet excited at the same time. I followed him to Venezuela, and now I am following him to this place. Memories of my mom and our adventures flood my mind, especially when we were driving along the highway. I begin reminiscing about what happened just weeks ago.

"The car is on empty," I say as I am driving her big white pickup truck. My mom is freaked out. She stammers out, "Oh no, what do we do? Annetta, the car is on empty! The car is going to stop!" I look down at the dashboard where the E for empty is glaring at me. "I know, let's pray!" As I pray, the stuttering car, about to stop, begins getting more power. We keep going. The vehicle should have stopped. "Lord, get us to a gas station," I say with desperation as we keep driving.

Soon, we are exiting onto a large hill. The car keeps moving. This has been going on for like 10 minutes. My mom's face says it all. Tears are flowing. We pull up to a gas station, and the car stops. I begin to cry. We just saw God do a miracle for us. God gets us to the gas station and shows us both that he is real.

A couple of years before this, I felt God tell me that we needed to stop at a particular store. The Holy Spirit was guiding me. I tell my mom, "God told me to stop here and go inside this store." She looks at me, bewildered, and questions me. "Let's go, I say with joy gleaming out of me." Just as I enter, I see my middle school Spanish teacher, whom I hadn't seen in years.

As I approach her, I apologize for how I had been in her class and share that I am now a Christian and sober. She was amazed and said, "I knew things would work out for you." My mom looks at me with tears and is completely in awe. I turn the corner, and there are others in the store whom I knew from my past, whom I was able to make amends with and share my testimony.

As we leave the store, proudly and lovingly, she says, "Annetta, God did this, and you did it." We saw God work together, which was a powerful experience for both of us. These moments were not only building my faith but also my mom's. God was showing us that He is real, and that people can hear His voice and obey.

A big bump, the car is moving fast over the road. My mind is brought back. I look around. This is it. This is where my new adventure will be. I look around at the muddy road. Mom looks at me with a longing to bring me back home with her. "Her eyes look into mine. Are you sure about this? With a worried look in her eyes. "Yes, this is what God wants me to do. As I get my things out, I hug her with the biggest hug I can. I feel her warmth and love. I know it's time to say goodbye.

I turn around and face the new life in front of me. As I enter, shuffling my things, the girls look at me and welcome me. Fear of the unknown takes my breath away. As I settle into my place, peace envelopes me and settles my soul. It now begins.

Chapter 28
-The Start-

I can't take it anymore. The claustrophobia is killing me. The room is closing in on me. I look for something familiar. There is nothing. My heart beats faster and faster. I feel faint. Is there anywhere to run? I don't know anyone here. I can't escape that night. I still feel like he's behind me. Waiting for me. It's been a few months, but I am still at that bus stop with my perpetrator. No one here gets it. Laughter fills the room. I am on the outside. I can't breathe.

My eyes scan the room for an escape. There it is. I swiftly move across the room, hoping to be unnoticed. I reach for the doorknob and climb the stairs. Finally, I can get away. Tears stream down my face. The sobbing begins. I haven't allowed myself to cry like this in so long. It is all coming out.

I hear someone coming. One of my new classmates tries to help me, but to no avail. "I'm getting Becky, the leader," she boldly says. My sobbing increases. I try to fight it, but I can't. Becky makes her way up the stairs. With each step, I know I will be found out. I came broken and am still broken. Becky looks at me with tender and compassionate eyes. "What's going on?" The words slip out of my mouth, barely making sense in between the sobs. "He attacked me," and the story comes out—more tears, more snot, more vulnerability.

She prays, and calmness enters me. "How about you join us downstairs?" "I don't want to," I mutter. It would be good for you, too. I make my way down, embarrassed by my tears. We finish our meeting and head back to the dorms. God is healing me, one encounter and one prayer at a time.

I am finding my way around this new place, and a friend says, "If you ever need a ride, there is a guy here who gives everyone a ride. Sometimes we all go to Walmart." "There he is," my new friend Rhonda points out. "Here, let me introduce you." I look at him in his oil-stained clothes. "Hey, Ryan, this is Annetta." She might need a ride sometime, says Rhonda. He shakes my hand. "Just let me know if you ever need a ride or anything," he says with kindness in his voice. "Ok, thanks."

Simone, my other friend, is always adventurous. Everyone knows Ryan as a taxi driver. "He can take us, that's how we can get a ride." "Fine, ok, let's do it. The concert was so powerful. I lift my hands and worship without any fear. The presence of God is overwhelming. Each song, I feel closer to Jesus. Ryan is there, and I am not afraid. I usually feel so awkward around guys, but I'm not around him.

"Do you want to get anything from Walmart, he calmly asks. Yes! How is this ok? We have gone with other people all the time, but now alone. Is this weird? I turn around and see him, and we laugh hysterically. Dress up at Walmart? I feel like a kid. This is so fun. I forget about my fear, my hurts, for a minute.

"Let's all go out for dinner; Simone says with joy in her voice—just me, Ryan, and Simone. We feel like the three amigos. We are always going out together after classes or on the weekend. People are talking. They look at me walking with Ryan, and the rumors are spreading.

Roger from my school yells out one day, "Hey, Mrs. Caldwell!" That's Ryan's last name; I realize with embarrassment. I yell with a red-stained face, "We are just friends!" I don't think of him as more than a friend. After all, Simone thinks he likes her, and he's not even my type. Rumors spread quickly in a small community.

It's been weeks since Simone approaches me. "Annetta, I think Ryan likes you and not me." "I only like him as a friend I say adamantly. "Well, you need to tell him how you feel. "You need to be honest with him." I know what I must do, but I don't want to hurt his feelings. I see him across the parking lot. "Here's your chance," Simone says, in all seriousness.

I slowly, sheepishly walk up. "Hey, Ryan! Can you talk for a sec? "Sure, he says. We walk to the picnic table. "So, I wanted to talk to you." I abruptly ask him if he likes Simone. No, he says. I like you. A dart pierces my heart. How do I tell him? "Well, I wanted to let you know that I only want to be friends." He looks at me with puzzled eyes. My heart hurts. Did I just hurt his feelings a lot? Well, at least I let him know. I find Simone and tell her. She looks at me, gleaming, "I am proud of you. I know that was so hard."

Chapter 29

-Thailand-

It's been a long three months. The classes have been difficult. I feel my heart is still broken. Am I really ready for this trip? At least I have been honest with Ryan, and at least I can have a break from drama. But as I realize the plane ride is here. Tomorrow, we leave for Thailand, and peace eludes me. My mind races to worst-case scenarios. "What if the plane crashes?"

As I enter the plane, I sit next to my quiet friend Susan. She is so calm. She holds my hand and prays. We invite Jesus onto this plane ride. Finally, after sixteen hours of this plane ride, we land and are done for now. I survived! I think to myself. I faced my biggest fear, and gratitude hits me.

The ride is bumpy. We all fit in this little pickup. Why aren't we told anything? The refugee camp is big and there are wires everywhere. The smell is strong. The people look tired and worn down. There are speakers with strange prayers going up. I am told those are for the Muslims. I can barely breathe—another hill to the village. The hill seems almost completely vertical.

The local women, with baskets on their heads, pass us up. We finally make it to our "home". The small woman and man glow with an overwhelming joy. Come and try our food. I have never seen such a big, beautiful smile. "How are they this happy?" I think, as she leads us into her tent home for a home-cooked meal.

The next evening, after playing with some local children, we gather on a small pickup. "Where are we going?" No one can tell us. It's late. We back the truck in front of the refugee camp. A small, nimble man appears. He runs and takes cover under the huge blanket. "Don't say a word," the leaders warn. The pickup is driving through low-hanging trees. We keep going for what seems like hours.

I feel the danger all around me. I don't know where we are or why we have taken this man from the camp. My thoughts turn as we finally reach our destination. The small man jumps out of the pickup as we stop. He leads us through the forest. I have to duck under the trees. The sounds are all around me—the buzzing of bugs and the swishing of mud underneath our feet. We keep walking until we see a large wooden picnic area.

I look to the left, and there I see a large lake, muddy and murky. The anticipation of what is happening is making me lightheaded. Where are we? As I look to the right, what is that? A soldier? Men begin walking their way towards us. Machine guns are wrapped around their shoulders and leaning towards the ground.

"What have I gotten myself into?" I muse. I see they march their way towards the skinny man we snuck out. He is a pastor! Before we know what is happening, the men remove their guns and begin to get baptized. We are here on a mission. A mission to help these men get baptized, as they have given their lives to Jesus. Excitement fills the air. The soldiers meet us with big, beautiful smiles on their faces.

Thank you, they say, as I realize we are part of something bigger than ourselves. As we finish and tuck the pastor back in the truck, exhaustion and exhilaration hit me. We safely sneak him back into the camp and make our way back to our netted beds.

Chapter 30
-Jumping despite-

"You look different, you seem happier." Everywhere I go, my friends from back home notice. My old boss lets me back to work. I am seeing how much God has done in my life. Just months ago, I left broken, confused, but determined to follow God. The money is coming in. God is giving me peace, all is well, until this one night. I can't sleep.

My heart is troubled. There's an impending doom hitting my heart. I make my way to my job. It's early in the morning. Suddenly, I hear it on the radio. Something major happens. What? Did an airplane hit a building? My boss rushes out the door and returns with a TV while moving around in hysteria.

The TV is loud, booming. Replay again. I see the plane hit the building. The news is being shared with pain and disbelief. The next plane hits the other building. Shivers move up and down my spine. Is this what I felt last night? Spiritually, I knew something wasn't right. The flames show. The building crumbles. The world is in complete chaos. How did this happen? My brain is still trying to comprehend it. How could this be? Tears pour down my face. Everyone is talking about it. How could this happen? Another plane hits the Pentagon.

My heart feels heavy. Why is this happening? Evil permeates the air. Should I have prayed harder last night? Could I have done anything? I know I couldn't have done anything. A still, small voice is still beckoning me to go, even after everything. I am supposed to go to YWAM? Days pass; I begin to tell others with a small crack in my voice. I believe I am supposed to go back.

My mom is shocked. You do see what happened? My leaders question me. Though I have changed for the better, why would I go out on missions right now? Because God is calling me. The days turn into weeks, and I, by some miracle, have enough money to go back at least for the schooling portion. Against all odds, I get back to YWAM and face another school called School of Evangelism (SOE), and another growing experience begins.

Sitting in class, thoughts of Ryan pop up. Am I running from this? Weeks pass. I am in class; I hear the teacher say something that reminds me of Ryan. This is the third confirmation that I think God might be saying Ryan is the one. I can't carry this anymore. My friend Melissa asks me how I am doing. "I think I have had three confirmations that Ryan and I are supposed to be together." Her face changes. She looks at me, concerned. "What are you going to do? I don't know," I reply.

Melissa can't hide her excitement. She is friends with both of us. Maybe she is secretly a matchmaker. She finds Ryan and, with a ray of sunshine in her voice, says, "Annetta has had three confirmations of you being together."

"Yes, this means the vision I had will come true." Just weeks ago, he was walking and praying. "God, I have these feelings for Annetta. Can I possibly date her?" Expecting a yes or no answer, to his surprise, the answer was much bigger. He sees me walking out to him and proposing. Quickly, the scene changes to me walking out in a wedding dress. "God, this is much bigger than what I was asking. I was just asking to date her." He starts telling his friends he likes me.

The next day, Melissa finds Ryan. "Hey, Ryan. I am so sorry, but with grief in her voice, Annetta says she doesn't see you two ever being together ever. A knife pierces his heart. As he begins to walk around the lake again, agitated, even angry, he prays out to God. God tells him, "I haven't released the feelings in her yet." He knows God's voice. Peace fills his heart again. "Ok, God, I am going to pray about this every day. He gets a journal, and with a newfound determination, he daily prays and marks the prayer in it. He will wait no matter how long it takes for his bride.

Chapter 31
-Match-Maker-

My other best friend, Jenni, is amazing. I can tell her anything. We are hanging out daily now, and Ryan is with us all the time. It's like a new three amigos is forming all over again. Seriously, Annetta, "What do you think about him?" asked Jenni, with wide eyes. "I just want to be friends, I say again. "Are you sure?"

Why is it that everyone sees us together? As I am walking, Ryan finds me. Hey! He says with a softness in his voice. "I was thinking maybe since you are missing Simone so much, maybe we can visit her for Thanksgiving when break comes up." Oh my gosh. Excitement fills my heart. "Yes, yes, let's do it, without fear of what others would think of us going alone on this trip. The day is finally here. Plans are made. Bags are packed, Louisiana here we come!

The trip up is so relaxing. I feel I can be myself with him. He's not judging me. I like being with him. Simone screams as we arrive. We have the biggest hug ever, and she leads me and Ryan into her cozy home. Her mom looks at me and hugs me intensely. And with a Louisiana twain, says, "Welcome to our home, let's get your bags put away. Dinner is delicious. As I make my way down the stairs, Simone and her mom begin the talk.

"Do you and Ryan like each other?" her mom asks with a slight grin. "Oh no, we are just friends, I say defensively. "Well, I have been watching him, and I can tell you right now, he likes you. If you don't like him, then you need to set things right. Let him know. This morning was so lovely. He made me breakfast, and I felt like I was home. It was a sweet moment. But I must push that away.

As Ryan comes out, I look at him and, with a boldness, I say, "We need to talk." We make our way to the back of the room, knowing I must once and for all let him know we are only friends. With a fire in my eyes, I look at him and say, "Ryan, we are only ever going to be friends. And we will never be together. The words burn as they come out of my mouth. I look at him, and there's peace in his eyes. He's not moved. Instant regret hits me.

I look at him and with all I can muster up, "Wait, unless well, have you heard anything from God?" He looks at me with curious eyes. "Actually, I have. And I have been praying about it for a while. He pulls out his book of prayers. I am sure all the color has drained from my face. Panic hits in. I get up, and Simone and her mom feel confused. Ryan is at peace and calm, and I am flustered, on the verge of sobbing.

The ride home is silent, depressing. I am not speaking. What do I say? I have made a fool of myself. I am angry. Though Ryan tries, all I do is grunt and refuse to talk.

It's a new day, and seeing Ryan, I run up to him and apologize. Can we just pretend that none of this happened? Can we just start over? "Sure, Ryan says, looking compassionately at me. I don't feel at peace. I feel anxious, almost like I have done something wrong. I am trying to be right with God, but it feels as if I am crying all the time. It's not just Ryan, I don't feel like anyone likes me in my school. I think my leaders don't believe in me, or I feel they judge me. I feel sad. I do not feel the same as I did when I finished DTS.

Christmas break could not come fast enough. I need a break. My friend's dad offers me a ride to my home for more fundraising. As we are leaving, Ryan runs up. "Hey, I made this for you." It's your favorite worship songs, and the cover is a picture of you praying." "Thank you," I say softly. My friend's dad looks at me as Ryan walks off. "Seems like a special guy to do that." Arriving at my friend's house is different this time. "Hey, you, ok?

Everywhere I go, I am looked at as if something is wrong with me. I don't sleep well. How am I going to fundraise? As I am battling my mind, soul, and spirit, I ask myself if I should even return to YWAM, and my friend approaches me. "You know, Annetta, there is always a consequence for our actions. I can't tell you if you should go or not, but there will always be a consequence. I feel God wants me to finish what I started in YWAM. I go to my room where I am staying. Close the door. Suddenly, as I gather my things, a picture of Ryan drops out. I look at it, and out loud I say, "he's not that bad looking, why am I running?"

My heart begins to soften. My friend Jake takes me to hang out. He is worried about me. We always pray for each other. As I am sitting in his car, I begin praying. I begin sobbing. And crying out, "God, would you give me a second chance, and would you undo all the flesh that I have fed over these last months? I look up, and I hear a voice, "It is finished."

And I feel something take something out of me. It is almost indescribable. I feel clean, fresh, new, and begin laughing. I can't control it. I hear God's audible voice. It is so booming, yet so loving and pure. Jake looks tenderly at me, like a big brother. "Do you want to get something to eat?" Yes, I say I am starving. As I am eating, it's like for the first time ever.

Everything tastes fantastic and is so fresh. After eating, I get up and share the gospel with a girl who is cursing nearby. I don't care what anyone thinks. I am in love with Jesus, and I must go back to YWAM. I know for sure now. I am so excited. I haven't slept. God provides a ride to the YWAM base. I feel different. I am different. God has given me a second chance, and I will not blow it this time. When I arrive, I need to find him. I must find him. With fire in my eye and love in my heart, I step out of the car....

Chapter 32
-Unexpected Blessings-

I find him. My eyes are warm and sparkling. "Hey, I didn't expect to see you here." I feel so much joy; I can't contain it. Everyone seems shocked when they see me. I left one way and came back another. "Can I use your computer I ask sweetly. As I check my email, I hear a small voice, "You are going to kiss him tonight." Ryan comes by me; would you want to go to a bonfire with some friends tonight and then to Lacy's house afterwards? Surprisingly, I say sure. It is New Year's Eve after all.

As he picks me up in his red pickup truck, things feel different. God is so close, and my heart is changed. The fire is bright and big, and the flames catch my attention. There is hollering and laughing. My mind is fully present and fully alive.

As we enter the truck, God is not done with me yet. I begin sobbing and crying out to God. Ryan doesn't know what to do. Should I leave her alone? he wonders. But God tells him to stay. I feel deep-rooted hurt begin to surface. God heal me. Take it all. I surrender it all to you, Jesus. What feels like hours begins to subside. Ryan looks at me patiently and says I think we need to head over to Claudine's house. I look up. As we are driving, gratitude for everything that God has done wells up inside of me. I am so thankful.

I begin thanking God for everything as a small child would. God, thank you for the trees. God, thank you for the clouds. God, thank you for......my New Boyfriend, or should I say fiancé. It was as if someone has taken control of my mouth. The words just came out of my mouth. Shock fills the car. Silence. My mind is spinning. What in the world did I just say? Ryan looks at me with his crazy thoughts. Did she meet someone on break back home? Is that why she is so happy? I look at him with a look of utter disbelief.

"Do you know what you just said? He stops the car on the side of the road. I look him in the eyes. An almost otherworldly feeling fills the car. We both realize it wasn't me who just proposed. It wasn't Ryan. It was the Holy Spirit himself. I look at Ryan and say, "What does this mean?" And with all seriousness in his face, the words echo in the car, "It means we are getting married!" An aroma of love fills the car as both of our lips touch, and a kiss like no other happens as the clock hits midnight.

We're Getting Married!

Chapter 33
-The Aftermath-

The drive to Claudine's house is sweet and exciting. Our first person to tell. As we come inside the small home, Ryan and I are smiling and giggling. Ryan is filled with awe, realizing that God has finally released my feelings. Claudine is suspiciously looking at us. "Ok, what has happened?" Ryan excitedly exclaims, "We are getting married?" Claudine looks at us in disbelief. She knows Ryan has been patiently waiting for me and that I have not been interested.

Her disbelief turns to joy as she looks at me and I say, "God did it," and relay our crazy encounter in the car. Emotions overwhelm me. Claudine calls one of her friends and shares the news. Ryan and I leave with our hearts full, excited about what God has done.

Ryan drops me off. I didn't want to say goodbye. I tell those awake what has happened. A giddy excitement fills the air. News spreads fast in our little community. Sleep evades me, as it has since I returned to YWAM. God has outdone himself.

The morning comes with butterflies shuffling in my stomach, now we walk and see Ryan waiting for me. Ryan hopes and prays that this is real. That last night is real to both of us. As he sees my entourage of friends giggling, walking in step with me, he knows his fears can be put at rest. He approaches me, and we walk. Hand in hand, we make it to the dock.

He gets down on his knee and asks me, "Will you marry me?" Though God started it last night, he wanted to finish it officially. "The words, "Yes! Come out of my mouth with a joy-filled smile. By now, the news had spread to everyone, including my leaders.

As I enter my class, my leaders look concerned. We know the rules. Students can't date staff members. He's officially a leader, and I am a student. Becky, my leader, makes eye contact. She finds me and, with a sternness in her voice, she says, "We need to talk." Ok, I say with trepidation in my voice. Did I do something wrong? I wondered. "I thought you were only friends. I thought you didn't have any feelings for him."

Becky's voice was one of concern, as if I were a young child being reprimanded. "I changed. My feelings changed. Something happened when I went back home." "Annetta, you can't go from only being friends to being engaged; it just doesn't work like that." My heart was beating faster. Were they saying this wasn't from God? I am so close to God right now, I ponder. I know his voice. And I know this is from him. "You barely know him, and you are still a student."

More meetings, more dramas. The next day, Dayson, the main leader of the school, schedules an emergency meeting. All hands on deck. The atmosphere is charged. First, Ryan goes in. Ryan shares in detail his vision, his heart, and what happened. Dayson's stern eyes meet Ryan's. His voice in a condescending way, "Well, I wish I could hear God like that, as unbelief fills the room. They all think we are crazy and that we aren't hearing from God, but our own thoughts.

Ryan exits, and I feel shaky. It's my turn to meet with Dayson. Dayson, in a fatherly way, tells me, "Annetta, tell me what happened. As I share the details of the night, his eyes look concerned. I tell him and Becky that this is real. This is God.

I catch them off guard with my insistence. "We must have a meeting about this. We will let you know what we decide. I turn to walk away, with fear knocking at my door again. It's unanimous. You guys must get to know each other first. It's only wisdom, you have to wait to get married.

The news shakes me. They were giving their permission, but it was like probation. "We are leaving on outreach soon, and Annetta can't be distracted or be a distraction to the other students. We agree to the terms. The days go by slowly, yet quickly. Ryan meets me often. "What kind of ring do you want?" I look at him, and my imagination begins to soar.

Roses! I want roses and begin to describe my ideal ring. "Ok, he says I will see what I can do, but that might be hard to find." The weeks go by, and we decide we need to pick a date for our wedding. We look at each other, bewildered. There are two dates we are looking at. "I don't know how to figure this out," I say, exasperated. Ryan looks at me daringly. "Why don't we both pray and ask God for a date? I agree.

I hear a date different than the other ones. I hear April 12th. I wait with anticipation. "Ok, I nervously ask, "What did you hear?" Ryan looks at me with a confused expression. "April 12th," he says, and declares it's not one of the dates we mentioned! Both of us are in shock. We both heard the same thing! Then that's it. April 12th will be our wedding date! We are excited that it will be a spring wedding! And yet we find out YWAM has a huge event planned for that day.

We wait knowing God will work it out. He always has. For now, we put it on hold, knowing my outreach day is here. I am in awe of what God is doing, yet trapped by man's approach to slow things down. I pack my things. The van is filling up. It's almost time. I see Ryan approaching the van. What does he have, I muse. He gets in the van. He walks towards me. He has something behind his back. What is he hiding?

He presents a gold-covered rose to me. The girls in the van exhale a sweet tone. I hear shouts from everywhere. "That is so sweet!" My heart melts. How can I be away from him for 6 weeks? We drive away, and as I peer out the van window, I see him waving affectionately as I wave too.

Chapter 34
-Jesus, My Everything-

"Don't get distracted", the prophetic leader says, as he approaches me. Everyone was falling when he got to them, but no one was afraid. My mind goes back to him. "Don't get distracted." I lose control over my body. What is happening? It's peaceful, but I am on the ground. I am looking up but not wanting to move. God is showing me how real and personal he is. It's time to come back. This church is so close to Jesus.

Ever since my experience back home, I feel so in tune and sensitive to God's presence. Worship begins. I close my eyes. I see him. I see Jesus. He approaches me. I look around. Does anyone else see Jesus? My eyes search the room. Everyone's eyes are closed.

I turn back and I hear it. "Don't be a Thomas. Don't doubt. Here touch my side. Touch my hands." Ok, I do. Ok, I believe. An Honor and a majesty hit. I just saw Jesus. I just interacted with him. Everyone already thinks I am crazy. But he is so real. I relish in what I just saw and felt. It goes deep in my soul. No one can take away what I just saw. It is permanently in my heart, in my soul.

Everything feels overwhelming right now. I miss Ryan. I miss hearing him. Finally, he calls. I hear his voice. I share my heart. I love to talk to him. I share my struggles of not connecting with the team, yet being so close to Jesus. "You will be ok, and I will see you soon." His voice comforts me. I go back to the team, ready to continue following Jesus.

I enter this new church. God's presence is so real. The overwhelming sense of God's bigness hits me. I slowly get on the floor. The fear of God strikes the room— the holiness of God. God have mercy on me. Forgive me for what is in my heart. I don't see this side of him often, but it is him. My heart feels as if it will explode.

Love rushes in along with a magnitude of his holiness and my lack of holiness. I feel different, I feel changed, but I need Jesus and a cleansing in my heart.

Church after church. Event after event. I am excited yet nervous about what each place will be like. The worship begins. I am overwhelmed by my sin. I cry loudly. I cry out for Jesus. I know I am loud. I can't help it. I am desperate for him. I know I am a little much, but I don't care. I want Jesus, and I want him to heal my heart. We all say our thanks to the pastor.

He begins encouraging me. I need this because I don't feel enough encouragement from my leaders or most of the other students. I tell him I love his painting of the woman Jesus washing one of the disciples' feet. He looks at me tenderly and says, "Do you want it?" I say yes, if, you are sure. He pulls it off his wall and hands it to me. God is showing me his love even when I don't feel it from others.

Finally, on our way home, my thoughts are again on Ryan and what God did before I left. I am so excited. He is waiting for me with anticipation. I greet him with a hug as all the girls are in awe of his love for me. A couple of days pass, Ryan finds me and asks to take me for a drive. "Sure, I say with my eyes glowing. The drive is familiar.

I realize that as we stop, it's where we first pulled over that night over a month ago. He has something for me. "Put out your hand, "he says softly.

He puts a ring, a beautiful ring, on my finger. The roses, I gasp. The ring is gorgeous. Tears fall as I realize that God does give me the desires of my heart. I am thankful I let God choose my husband because God really does know best.

Chapter 35
-Love Restore All Things-

Could it be true? Not only is God giving me a husband, but he is also giving me dance back. I let dance go to follow Jesus when I left to do missions. I didn't know how it could come back. But here it is. The School of Performing Arts (SOPA). A school here at YWAM that focuses on dance. I had to do DTS first, and now I am ready. I am learning various dance styles, including hip hop, classical, and lyrical—all of it for his glory. My heart leaps. God, you are amazing. God wants even more freedom and healing in my heart.

SOPA Dance

I feel God tugging at my heart. The teacher looks at us with a beckoning. The project will force me to face my fears and the hurt again, and to be vulnerable to such a depth within me. It's my turn to share. My feet feel as if they are dragging. I show my picture. It has a girl longing for purity. There are doves on it. She looks battered.

As I hold up the picture, I share. I share the shame. I begin sharing the experience, how I was almost killed before coming to YWAM. I share my feelings. The tears and pain and agony of everything I have gone through make their way up my throat and out for everyone to see. I was ashamed in my last school for being too vulnerable. This is risky, but I know God is saying to do this. As I finish, my heart feels as though it will pop out of my chest, and I sit with a mix of embarrassment and joy that I obeyed God. One of the leaders, with tears in her eyes, invites me back up.

She feels led to pray for me, and the entire group prays. What is this feeling? Is that healing? Bubbling up inside of me, pain turns into love. Hurt and bruising are turning into softness and life. She turns to me, as I am in front of the whole class. "Annetta, do you want to be free from this? Do you want to give this to God? I say yes. She grabs a zip lock bag and says, "Put some of your artwork in this bag and come with me."

It appears as a scene from a movie. Like soldiers on a mission, we make it to the lake. "Now throw it into the lake and let this go to remember no more." I gather all I can in me, and as this group is my witnesses, I take the bag and throw it into the lake. The burden lessens. I feel free. She proclaims, "Annetta, this is no longer your identity. You are free! God has taken this from you." The powerful moment is etched in my mind and heart forever. God is healing me, truly healing me.

Ryan and I prepare for outreach as an engaged couple. We go to Hollywood and all over California, sharing hope with others through dance and testimonies. Performing on the streets of Santa Monica, I notice twin girls with long curly hair, wearing leather jackets, dancing close by.

In that moment, I feel the Lord whisper to me, "Those are your future daughters." I know that whisper. Wonder fills my heart as I watch them closely. How could that be? I have always been afraid of having children. My mind brings me back to holding my nephew. Fear consumes me as I proclaim I will never have children.

I was scared. The thoughts of going through childbirth consumed me. Jolted back to reality, I look expectantly at the twin girls. Is that joy I feel? Maybe, just maybe, I would like to have children. Ryan is nearby, noticing the twin girls too. Little did I know God was speaking to him, too. He quickly takes a picture to record this moment. God is speaking to both of us. In our own way, separately.

Another day passes. We enter a little white colored church. It is small, but God's presence is thick here. We all gather and find our seats. The seats are tightly close to each other and are hard chairs. The air feels light. The worship begins. It's sweet, inviting to my tired body.

To my surprise, the speaker looks right at me. "Stand up." He looks right at me. I turn around. He couldn't be talking to me. The room spins. "You, yes, you stand up." I get up slowly in embarrassment, wondering why he would look at me. "God has called you to dance.

When you dance, people will be set free. God has given you this gift, and it is for glory." Could he be speaking to me? I am just an average dancer. I am sure there are more qualified dancers, I think to myself. I nod in agreement, but my mind races as thoughts of others more qualified than I, who should receive this word, like Lynn.

Lynn is the lead dancer. She is so humble and yet causes others to be in awe as the spirit of God moves in her. Her delicate frame screams, dancer! She would be the natural choice for such a word.

I am built differently. Not heavy, just not delicate. I am a side dancer, not even chosen to dance solo or even to dance with the excellent dancers. Dancers in this room surround me. Is this really for me? The tears fill my eyes, and peace envelopes me. I know this word is for me, even as unworthy as I feel. The words begin to go down into my heart where I receive this unlikely gift, packaged from heaven, custom-fit just for me.

Chapter 36

-Hurt Again-

I open the door. I see them. Everyone. We just met, I remember Brianna. She was there for me during SOPA. Brianna is the life of the party. Everywhere she goes, people come to life. I turn; there's Rolinda. But it's different. SOPA was different. Laughing continues. Why am I on the outside?

My nerves are raw. Anyone hear me? Oh good, Ryan steps by me and puts his comforting arm around me. Today is a new day, Shyness overtakes me. A wall of protection covers me. Why am I here? I know how to dance, so why can't I dance on the stage? Fear, is that you? I remember this feeling. Rejection? I felt this before. I felt it a lot in my life. Lies form.

Maybe I am not good enough to be here. "She is always talking about pink, and I can't believe she said that." The words continue as I run into the bathroom. Are they talking about me? My mind races, and daggers of rejection penetrate. I cannot stop the tears, and the cries are getting louder.

Suddenly, I hear a knock on the door. Annetta, what's wrong? they ask genuinely. My voice cracks. "I know you were talking about me." My voice is heavy with hurt. "No, we were talking about someone else! I promise you." I look around. I know I have to come out. Sheepishly, I open the door. Katrina hugs me and assures me that they were not talking about me and that they like me. My face burns hot with embarrassment. Temporarily, I believe her, maybe I am liked on this team even though it is no SOPA.

God, I pray, "Why bring me on this team? I don't feel loved. I feel insecure here." My mind is drawn back to reality. "Let's get a group picture! The group piles on each other. My body wants to run and be with them, but fear of rejection makes my feet stick to the ground like rocks. No one invites me. The moment is over. Tears fill my eyes. Too late. It's now the boy's turn. Ryan runs up there without any hesitation. Belonging. I remember feeling that. Just months ago, I thought I belonged in my school of the arts. I didn't hold back. I wasn't left out. I was loved. Here? It's different. I guess I am expected to push my way in. But I can't.

Another trip. Another drive. Ryan drives most of the time. He doesn't struggle. He just likes to be with people, quiet yet engaged. A voice from the back begins telling a joke. All are listening. I try to understand. It goes over my head. Laughter again fills the van. Why can't I fit here? I hear it again, "You are rejected. Nobody wants you here." You aren't liked. The lies fill my mind, as if a demon has been whispering into my ear. The demon's voice gets louder and louder, "No one likes you. You shouldn't be here."

We are in a new town. The whole team loves this new couple. Well, I think to myself, she probably won't talk to me. She approaches me with a lightness in her step and love in her countenance. "Hey, I hear you are getting married. Tell me all about your dress." As I describe the dress I am borrowing from a friend, my voice falls flat. "It's ok, I guess." Looking at me in all seriousness, "Then it sounds like you didn't find your dress yet. There should be excitement and joy in it. Do me a favor, pray about the dress, and maybe you can get someone to make it."

My eyes light up! Yes, I want butterflies and a flowy dress, and I stammer something beautiful." I feel a touch of acceptance that carries me through, and I determine to get a new dress.

Betsy approaches me. She loves red. I love pink. A fun competition begins. I feel she is one of the few friends I have on this team. She knows me from SOPA. Without Betsy, I don't know what I would do. She says, "Let me help you with your hair." She is so motherly. She gently pulls me out of my comfort zone.

Do you want to do this dance with me? I look at her with fear in my eyes. Me dance? Just us on the stage?

Most of the time, it has been a group of us. I manage to get a yes out shyly. The dance is beautiful. She believes in me. I feel a moment of acceptance. Maybe I can fit in. The feeling eludes me as I get back with the team, and once again left out of most conversations. But at least I have a moment of being seen.

We arrive safely home to the YWAM base. The leader Fred is so nice to me. Fred, Ryan, and Betsy make me believe I am worth being a part of this team. I approach him and ask if the team can help with our wedding. He says, absolutely, with resoluteness in his voice. As we gather in a group, my heart beats faster. Fred says, "Annetta has a request for us." The words are like molasses, yet forceful, almost demanding. "I want you guys to help with my wedding."

Why didn't I ask nicely? Full of fear, nothing comes out right. Silence fills the air. Kindly, Fred says, "Come on, guys, we can help, right?" The yes comes sporadically. Ok, now we can focus on wedding planning, and my heart begins to feel a bit of joy with anticipation.

Chapter 37
-The Big Day and Beyond-

The smell of the nail salon fills my nostrils. A buzz of activity is in the air. I am the center of attention. "We must make her look perfect; it's her wedding day!" My nails are being etched into perfection. I look around, my mind filling with wonder. For a moment, anxiety strikes, and I quietly ask, "How much is all this costing?" She gently smiles, for you, nothing. You must be one loved girl because your friend over there paid for everything." Aghast, I look over at my friend and smile and mouth, "Thank you."

My hair and makeup are now being done. Sparkles shine on my face. I wonder to myself, this must be how Esther felt. Love is reaching into my heart. The hurt from mobile teams is subsiding. I think back to this past month. As they are helping with flowers, with songs, with everything to make this a perfect day. Maybe I am wrong. Maybe they do like me.

Joy is flowing into every spot of my heart. So many are coming to celebrate our wedding. As I walk into the house to continue getting ready, I see my reflection. I look beautiful, and my heart feels beautiful. But I am told one thing. "You can't walk barefoot on the hill." Panic fills my eyes. My sister, in a rescue mission along with some bridesmaids, says we don't have time! I sprint towards the car.  With my hair all done, we race the clock to the nearby mall. We run through the mall proclaiming it's my wedding day and I need shoes.

No one has the shoes we need. Finally, we approach the last store. There they are—the most beautiful sparkly flip-flops. Without hesitation, we buy them and run back to the wedding as fast as we can. Whispers fill the room. Where were you? Your wedding is going to start soon. As we tell them, relief washes over me, and I can prepare once again. A friend approaches me. "Annetta, look out there. This is all for you. Look at what God did." I look out at the chairs and feel God's smile at me as I prepare for this moment.

The room is spinning with excitement. There's a sweet fragrance in the air. The walls are white. The chairs are closely placed together. I find rest for one more moment. As I put the dress on, I sense the delight of Jesus. Gratitude is all I feel. A friend suggests praying over me. "Let God be glorified." All hands are laid on me. Prayer after prayer, I know this moment will be etched in my mind forever. I know in my heart that God  will show up and show off to my family—especially those who don't know him.

My dad approaches me. "It's time." As he puts his arm out and we walk to the hill, fear tries to pop up. My dad whispers, "You are going to be ok."

The music begins. My time is coming. The friends from the mobile team are in front of me. They have their swords raised. The fabric from the last two swords is hiding me as if waiting for the big reveal. It feels as if angels are with me, escorting us down the steep hill; it feels like I am stepping into a beautiful, redemptive story.

The song is playing. The lyrics seem to shout, "there will be no more fear or pain, representing Jesus walking with me. In this moment, it's as though I am marrying not only Ryan but also entering a deeper union with Jesus. This is God's glory. His love story of redemption. The prayers are being answered. "God gets the glory."

Worship begins. Songs play as if heaven is open on this huge field. My hands extend towards the sky. Eyes closed, I feel God near me. Tears fall. God is so good. He did it. He is so faithful. Ryan begins washing my feet, and I feel as if God is showing me true love. And my own sin being washed away. God has purified me, and I am his. And now I am Ryan's, too.

The vows are done, and the rumble is heard behind us. Fireworks fill the air. Am I dreaming? The beauty of colors filling the sky, Ryan, with a gleam in his eye, picks me up. Joy and grace fill my heart. My eyes catch a glimpse of the hill. "What is that?" Everyone is pointing at the hill. A big horse-drawn carriage with long, beautiful lights come gallantly down the steep hill. My breath is taken away. I feel as if I am in a storybook with God redeeming my life. Could this be for me? Really, for me? God is answering every detail, every prayer. We race with giddiness towards the carriage, and all our bridal party gathers aboard.

I enter with the announcement, Welcome, Mr. Ryan and Mrs. Caldwell. The sound was so sweet to my ears. I have never felt such peace in my life. God is writing my story, and it is a good one.

Every song, every conversation, is filled with grace, gratitude, awe, and wonder.

Where are we going? We enter the bed and breakfast. The night is pure and redeeming. God has restored me. I am pure. I feel as if I am having a second chance at life. We pull up to the Precious Moments' hotel. I see precious moments everywhere. Ryan knows me so well. God is giving me the desires of my heart. The shows are fun. I don't have a care in the world. Only Ryan and Jesus are here.

I guarantee you; the next place is going to be better than this one. "How could that be possible? We come to a sign. Iowa. "What could be Iowa?" I question with skepticism. As we drive on the long road leading up to something, my curiosity is piqued. "Where are we?" Just wait and see, Ryan says with excitement in his voice. The scene plays out. A huge castle appears. As if things could not get any better, I cry out, "No Way!!!"

The suit of Armor fills the hallways. The room is beautiful. In the middle of the large room, a royal bed is pristinely made. The room exudes royalty. The peace of God envelopes me. I am a princess, and I am with my prince. More stairs lead to an overlook of trees and farmland. How could I get this blessed? God whispers a love song to me. I close my eyes and let the wind blow my long flowing hair as I lean over and look deeply into my beloved's eyes.

Chapter 38

-Back on the Road and a Little Surprise-

I never want this to end, I think to myself. I have never felt so much fulfillment, so much peace as these last six weeks. But alas, it is time. The mobile team was waiting for us. This time we will be on it as an official married couple. Fear knocks on my door. Old feelings crop up. Fear of having children. I know I will have children. I remember the twins. I must overcome this fear.

Just take the test, Annetta. What if I am pregnant? Panic floods my mind. I heard about pain in childbirth. I can't do this. I take the plunge. The test shows up. Pregnant? It is true. I am pregnant. Joy and fear collide. I share the news with worry in my voice.

Why aren't you happy? Ryan is nervous. It's so soon. We have only been married for 6 months. Our plans were different. Wait five years and then start having children. We are still on the team. What do we do? How will this work? We only do what we know to do. We pray. Fear begins to be choked out by the wonder and happiness of the little one inside of me. The pictures of her bring exhilaration. Our first baby. Every appointment. Every detail. She is wonderful. The flutters begin.

I feel as though I can see God forming her in my womb. She is fearfully and wonderfully made. Though fear of childbirth is still there, something is changing in me. Every episode of throwing up, every appointment. Every test. It reminds me that I have something special. A special gift is growing inside of me. God speaks to us both. Her name is Sarah. Her name means princess.

I am walking around the YWAM base, my belly getting larger by the day. My friend Clarisa greets me. Hey, Annetta, can I pray for you and your baby? Of course, I say. She lays her hands on my belly and begins the words. "Your daughter will be a prophet. She will see things as black and white." Do not worry about her, this is how I made her." As she finishes blessing her, tears wet my face. I know deep in my heart; there is something special about her. God is going to do something big in her life one day.

As calm as can be, the words gently glide out of my mouth. "My water just broke." Ryan awakened from sleep. "Are you sure?" Yes, I say without hesitation. "Well, I guess we should get our bags. The lack of emotion was humorous. As we arrive, my midwife calmly checks us out. Hours pass. She is taking her sweet time. Pain in each contraction, my midwife reminds me that I will be meeting our sweet baby soon. The sounds of Finding Nemo playing on the TV temporarily distract me.

I must walk. The walk is getting harder. It's time. I am pushing and pushing, but she doesn't come out. I have been pushing for almost three hours. My body is drained and tired. Finally, we are here. I feel God's presence as we are playing my favorite worship songs. I am facing my fear head-on. Just one more push, Annetta. She's hardly crying. The chord is wrapped around her neck. The doctors come and help. After what seems like a lifetime, she is finally placed on my chest.

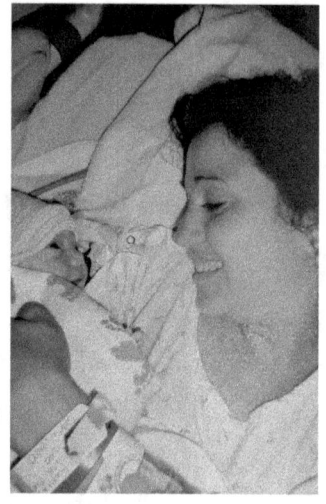

I say it to myself, God, how could I ever not trust you after this? I feel as if I am in a dream as I look at Sarah's face. She appears to look up at me, as if to say, "Are you my mama?" My heart opens in a way I didn't know existed. Joy and peace surround me.

The next day, our mobile team shows up. They fill the room with at least 30 people. I feel love and I feel belonging. God is healing every part of me.

Chapter 39

-Back on the Road, Take Two-

"She is still so little, I don't know if we should bring her on the road." Back and forth and many prayers later, we decide, ok, we will bring little Sarah on the road with mobile teams. Finally, we are here. Next week we head out. Uggghh, I don't feel so well. Maybe it's just from having Sarah and how tired I am. Every day, I feel a little worse, and here comes the throwing up. I can't be. Can I? Ryan, we should take a test. There it is two dark lines. I am in awe but freaked out! Sarah is only 6 months old, and we are leaving soon. All bags are packed, and we are ready. "Now remember, don't say anything to anyone." We must keep this a secret. You are way too early on to share.

Every stop becomes increasingly difficult to hide. The toilet is my new friend. "Annetta, are you ok? My vomiting is easy to hear from miles away. As our eyes meet, my friend's eyes meet mine. "Annetta, are you pregnant? A strange smile forms on my face. The cat is out of the bag, and there's no catching it. The trip gets harder, but I know we are supposed to be here.

This church is amazing. We talk about warfare. I know I am pregnant, but I must dance. I will be ok, right? As I finish, I am noticing something strange. What is that? Panic sets in. There is fluid leading out. Why would this happen? In the bathroom, I ask a friend if it's normal to have fluid leaking out this early in pregnancy. "I don't think so, she stammered.

Ryan, though injured from a cut, gets me to our host home. We pray. I know something is wrong. Tell the team to pray, I say with urgency. In no time, the team shows up. They ask for God's mercy and his grace. "God, please spare this child's life." I am crying, feeling as if it's my fault. Peace falls in the room. The fluid begins to slow. The pain subsides. When I talk to the doctor, they say as long as it stops, you are ok.

I know God spared Hannah's life, and I am so very thankful. We finally make it back home to our sweet home that we bought. Prayers continue. This lady knows how to pray. She looks at me and says, "You will have an easy delivery. Blessings, blessings. Your kids will not have to go through what you went through." The words go deep. This prophecy is straight from God to me. I hold on to them.

I have finished the race of mobile teams. Finally, I can stay at home. I can relax and prepare. Every doctor's appointment is good. Again, thankfulness fills my heart as Hannah is ok and still with us. I thank God for his grace. As we arrive at the doctor's office, I remember my Hello Kitty doll. Let's put it on the table and see what she does. As she enters, laughter erupts at the sight of the dishevelled doll on her table. Alright, alright, do you want me to check you? She snickers; it's not like you will be in labor.

As she checks me, her eyes widen, and in shock, she proclaims, "You are in labor. You need to head to the hospital." I manage to get my last meal in at the mall. As we leave, a lady asks how far along I am, with a big grin, "I am in labor now!" Only three hours later, my beautiful Hannah is born. We turn on our 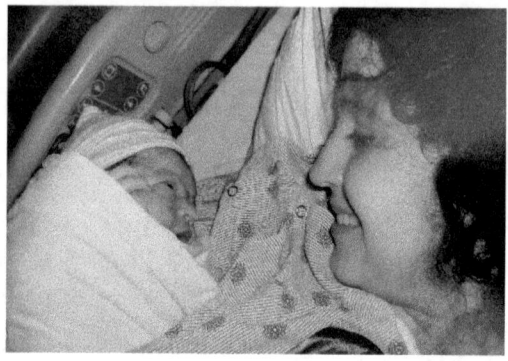 favorite show, Amazing Race, and I get my favorite meal, a yummy hamburger. Again, in awe of God's faithfulness, I cuddle with my girl, so thankful that she is here with us.

Chapter 40
-Shock-

The room is cold and white. The sterile environment only adds to my panic. Each step closer leads to the fear of the unknown. The pain in my stomach is intermittent. The blood is still coming out. Pain shoots through my body as I realize things might not be ok. An older man comes into the room as I sit on the cold, comfortless hospital table. I am bold as I look at him, "I am so sorry, but I don't want to see a man." Confused, he leaves the room as a tear forms on my sleep-deprived face.

The nurse makes her appearance. "I am sorry, but this man is the only one we have on duty, and he is a good doctor. You are in good hands." I crumble inside. Not only am I possibly losing my baby, but now a man must examine me? Panic and worry consume me. I begin to cry uncontrollably. "Let's get this done quickly," he says. Then the picture appears on the screen.

The baby is visible, perfect, and mine. "Is he ok?" I forget about my discomfort. "It looks like he has only developed to 6 weeks, and he should be 9 weeks." His voice feels far away and echoes. I feel as though I am out of my body. My mind can't handle the news. The picture burns into my brain and can't ever be erased. "You will most likely bleed more and then pass the baby; there is a chance that things can be ok, but only time will tell."

He looks into my hurt, painful eyes and tries to find a feeble attempt to comfort my grieving heart. "It's not that bad, at least you have two healthy babies at home." His callous words echo in my mind. Is there no emotion in his heart? Anger and pain are buried deep inside of me. I can't catch my breath. I try to bring hope in. "Maybe the baby will be ok," I say as I look at Ryan. He tries to help, quietly, so it comes out correctly from his hurting heart. We both know what this likely means. He holds my hand. Our drive home is silent. It's unlike our other doctor's visits. This one is painful. Our hearts are being torn as the reality of the news hits us.

A day passes, and as the doctor said, the bleeding will continue, and you will pass the baby. The pain is sharp. The contractions continue until I feel it. Something comes out. I know it's my baby. I investigate the toilet, blood filling it with remains of our precious baby. The pain is so deep I can't handle it. God help me, I cry out. The pain ripples into the air. Thankfully, someone is watching our other kids. In a whirlwind of emotions, we pray. We both feel it. We both think it. This was a boy. Our boy. We want to honor him. What would we have named him? To my surprise, we agree, his name was Daniel. My sweet Daniel. The next day, with pain in our eyes, we have a funeral for our boy. Though Sarah and Hannah are young and confused, I want them there to say goodbye to their brother.

Chapter 41
-Rainbows After Storms-

I walk into the bright room. Laughter and voices are loud. Don't they know what I have gone through? Don't they know how much pain I am in? The awkward stares, the silence. Either no one knows what we just went through, or they don't know what to say. I lightly speak to my friend, "We are struggling, you know, since having the miscarriage." A blank stare. "I didn't know," she says, obviously uncomfortable. Why did I say that? I just guess I want to be acknowledged. To have some sympathy. Something, anything.

I hear it. Will you praise him in any circumstance? Will you praise him still? Even in the pain? I lift my hands heavy with grief. I decided even here, where I feel betrayed by him. I would still praise him. Why, God, why would you allow us to have him only a little while and then take him away? Why allow me to experience this pain?

It hurts too much. One moment, I am fine. The next moment, I feel I will drown in my grief. I still remember the pain, the life that was lost. But I will still praise you. The days are blurring together. I love these two girls. Sometimes I feel like my heart will explode.

I look at them and I outline their faces in my mind. Sarah and Hannah are the best gifts. Ryan is here with me. I am so thankful he wakes up to change them and checks on me. They didn't say it would still be this hard. Joy and heartache are all mixed in. Weeks turn into months. What is that familiar feeling? Why am I so tired? I don't feel good. Maybe? Could it be? The test feels longer than usual. What will I do if it's positive, I quip at Ryan. I don't think I can do this again. "One day at a time," he says lovingly. I can't look. As I look for a hint from Ryan, he gives nothing away. Seconds feel like an eternity. "Congratulations!" he says with a grin as big as the sun. Oh my gosh, I get to have another baby! Excitement fills the air. Excitement mixed with fear. Lord, please let him be ok.

I look out at our beautiful land, filled with trees and trails. I can envision our kids growing up here. The forts they will build, the dirt they play in, and all the fun we will have. My dream is abruptly shaken. Months ago, there was talk about moving to be with our mobile team leader in Virginia. He would have a job for Ryan, and we could be well taken care of. Of course, I said no. I want to live our life here, but I prayed. Here I am, pregnant with a new baby, Samuel. I can't travel while pregnant. Or so I thought.

The pull was getting greater. My new small group leader, with wide eyes, looks at me. "You know, Annetta, maybe God is calling you out there, to live a life with a job. A normal life? Calling me back? My defensive eyes dart at her, "I have finally accepted that I will be a long-term missionary. I have said yes to God, so why would he now want me to leave missions in YWAM? Have I failed him somehow? "No, sometimes God calls us to new things." I look down and solemnly say, "I will pray about it."

The prayers are unending: "God, if you want us to go, please speak to us." We both feel it. We both know it. It's crazy! Ryan goes to visit Virginia to check things out. As he returns, we both know it's time to move on from YWAM and onto this next adventure in Virginia.

We pack our bags, we list our house, and we jump. The truck is full of all our things. The memories of this home fill my mind. This is our first home. This is where Sarah and Hannah were raised. This is where my Daniel is buried. Memories of God's faithfulness to us are tangible. As I step into the truck, it's almost as if a fresh wind of God's presence falls on me. The peace is so thick. I know we are supposed to leave, but it's hard to say goodbye.

Sometimes God calls me to leave the familiar for something better. I look at the house we have called home, one last time. I try to sketch it in my mind so that I won't forget. I look at my large 8-month-sized pregnant belly, and with a child-like faith, I say Let's go. Virginia, here we come.

Chapter 42
-Hardship with Grace-

Panic fills my heart. Where will I deliver Samuel? Will the church give us insurance? We don't have the money to pay for the baby. Cynthia, one of Ryan's co-workers, looks at me calmly. "You will be taken care of, trust God. He indeed brought us all this way; God won't drop us now. Every day, I am getting closer to Samuel's arrival. I am waiting with anticipation. Will we be covered? Will we have a hospital to deliver in? The call comes. "Yes, we will cover your wife for childbirth." I exhale a sweet sound of relief. This church is so good. It is different, but I somehow feel at home. I feel peace here.

The contractions begin. They are getting closer and closer. Ryan's parents are thankfully here. This is it. The drive is sweet. I wobble my way through the back doors. This hospital is new. God let it go well.

The labor is slow but steady. The blankets and heater come in. We know it won't be long now. I push, driven by great determination, knowing we will see my son soon. As the nurse places him on my chest, I know it. Again, God has been faithful to us.

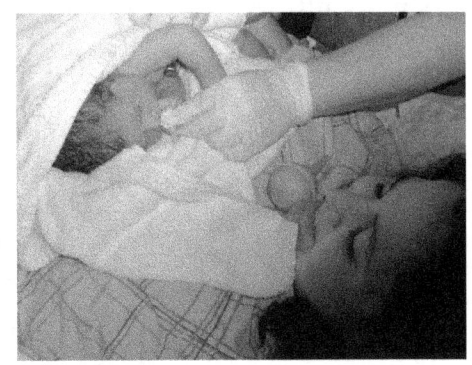

We moved in obedience from Texas, and now we have a healthy baby boy. I look at Ryan with awe. God has helped us again." I am blown away. Joy and peace replace the months of anxiety and fear. Thank you, Jesus, for hearing our prayers.

Now at home, why am I not feeling right? It's been 3 days since I gave birth to Samuel. Anxiety fills my mind. My body hurts more than usual. My throat is hurting. Maybe I am just tired from giving birth and all the stress of moving. Ryan knows something isn't right. We find a sitter for our other kids and walk through the doors of the unknown clinic.

The environment is heavy, a sick feeling. "I don't want to be here." I turn to look at Ryan. Anxiety is filling my mind. What if something is seriously wrong? The doctor strolls in. With a somber voice, "Unfortunately, it looks like you have contracted Mono." Mono? What the heck. How could I have contracted Mono? I just gave birth 3 days ago. The doctor looks at me plainly, "You probably contracted it from the hospital."

We gravely left the clinic, knowing that it takes a long time to recover, and I had three children to care for now. Thankfully, I had Ryan's parents' help. Though it is still hard, I am so thankful to feel better now.

Chapter 43

-Good News-

The phone rings. Yes, that's my name. "I have some good news for you." We have a buyer for your house in Texas!" My heart is overwhelmed. We have been waiting over 2 years to sell our Texas house. "She has offered a full price offer for it, and you don't even need to come here to get it done. "Seriously, we don't have to go there?" How good is this? Ryan agrees, and she is sending paperwork over. I am shaken. God has once again taken care of things. And just in time since I was pregnant once again.

"I don't like that one. The house is literally falling apart." The agent hesitantly shows us another one. Well, this one has termite damage. Ok, maybe this one will be good. We drive through the tall grass. Warning signs are up. Don't trespass. Be aware. Yikes, I don't have any peace here. It's scary. "Let's look at another house."

"I have another one in your price range, but it's a twin house. It's connected just at the garage, though. Hmm. I don't like the thought of that, but I am willing to see it at least. The sidewalk leading to the house is pretty. The home is stable, much better than the others. As the door opens, I notice something missing. Oh, wait, no stair rail. The fixtures on the ceiling are missing. It has a reasonable frame, but it will take a lot of work.

The backyard is decent. Hmm. Upstairs we go. I open the door to one of the kids' rooms. "What is that other door?" I ask curiously. "Oh, that's a bonus room!" the agent says with enthusiasm. I open the bonus room door, and a light in my heart goes off. We already prayed and knew we wanted to homeschool our kids, and this would make a beautiful schoolroom. I look around with delight. "Yes, yes, yes! This is our home. Ryan is just as excited. Yes, I think this is our future home.

She will let us know that she will prepare a special loan offer so that we can finalize it. I am speechless. This is it. God has given us a new home after being in the apartment for so long. The bid is given, and now the waiting begins.

Every ring of the phone, we think this is it. Nothing. Why is it taking so long? The wait is torturous. I can hardly stand it. Finally, the phone rings again. Ryan's face drops. The house has already been sold to someone. My heart aches. The clock is racing against us. We can't have this many people in a two-bedroom apartment.

How are we going to possibly find a home in time to give birth to our new baby? I guess we just have to keep looking. Nothing is standing out. We keep praying. Just when all hope seems lost, the agent calls again. "Are you ready for some good news?" The person who put in a bid did it illegally. Your bid is the next in line, and they are accepting yours. My heart feels as if it will burst out of my chest. This means I get the homeschool bonus room. We get a loan that will help us rebuild the house. And this is just in time for our new baby girl.

This girl is going to be named Abigail. I am having another baby! I want a different hospital to deliver Abigail at. However, this other hospital demands that I get the Rh-negative shot since my blood type is A-negative. Since Ryan and I both have A-negative blood, I don't need the shot. They don't believe I have the same father for this many kids. I must find a hospital that respects my wishes. Will DePaul have a midwifery center? Sign me up now. Every tour, every detail is perfect for us.

I arrive ready to do this. I have a new sense of accomplishment. We have a home to go to; God is answering so many prayers.

The time comes, and as I am pushing, the nurse looks at me in an endearing tone. Remember to look at her face when she comes out. When you look at a baby first coming out, it's like looking at the face of God. There is such purity with the baby. She quickly shows her to me 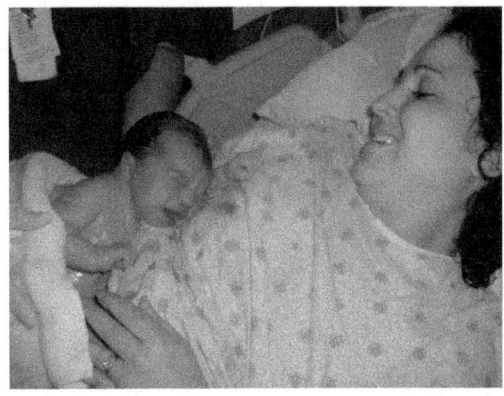 right after, and I am filled with awe and wonder. She places Abigail on my chest, and peace fills me. As I am in recovery, they let us rest for 6 hours. My heart is content.

Chapter 44

-Hurry Up and Slow Down-

She looks at me blankly. My legs begin to shake. Why am I so nervous? I have done this so many times before. This is baby number five. "Will it hurt?" I ask. The midwife, Linda, ready to laugh, looks at me squarely in the eyes. "Will it hurt? Of course, it will. You have done it before." Her voice is irritated, almost angry. Maybe it was because months before this moment, I heard the doctor's words but didn't want to believe her. Your baby is breech. Breech? My baby is facing up instead of down. Up until now, things have been going well.

What should I do, questioning everything? I didn't want to have surgery. Lord, please help me. We pray, and we know what we have to do. Let's go to the chiropractor. "Is there anything that you can do?" I ask incredulously. The chiropractor doesn't seem concerned. He looks at me and begins to feel around my stomach. Yes, there you are!" We can move her after we loosen this muscle.

It will take some time, but I think we can do it. I don't care as long as I can get her unbreeched. "Lord, please help me", I whisper. The pain begins, the pressure. A little at a time, and the muscle starts to relax.

I feel the turning. The room becomes smaller as I try to breathe. We have done all we can today. Come back tomorrow, he says with confidence. We do not want to put you or the baby through too much at once. I walk through the doors, confident and hopeful that we will not have to have a C-section.

Again, the chiropractor gently moves my baby. She begins turning. The baby is turning! Everyone is so happy. The technique is working! I have hope it will work. I am so thankful. I walk through the bright doors. My midwife greets me, but still with worry, knowing that my precious Rachel was breech last time I came in.

Her eyes widen as she examines me. Her head is down! She can hardly believe it, but relief is in her eyes. It was just in time. Now I can still have a natural delivery! Thank you, Jesus! He is constantly answering our prayers, and this was another big one.

My mind finds its way back to the room. The midwife Stacy again questions my sanity as I continue to be anxious. In her desire to leave early, she earnestly looks at me. Do you want to get this done quickly? Surprised by her question, I answer yes. As I lay on the uncomfortable bed, she tells me to push. Push? But I don't feel the urge to push. I have done this four times before. I know what pushing feels like. She again insists. Exhaustion is my constant companion now. Stacy looks concerned but has to leave. I am sorry, but my shift is over. Olivia will be here soon.

Olivia arrives and looks at me. I want to be done; I say with a tired whisper, "I want an epidural." She tenderly looks at me, "Let's check you out first. Oh my gosh, you are completely swollen down there." I told her that Stacy told me to push, and now she looks dreadfully at me. We all know she should not have told me to do that. Ryan and I are praying and calling others on his phone to pray as I am wheeled towards the main hospital.

Panic is setting in. Crying tears of fear and worry, I beg for them to hurry. Suddenly, I feel pressure. The baby's heart rate drops. Olivia looks at me. In a stern voice, she warns me that this is serious. I am thrown aggressively onto my back, as they all see something. Rachel's head is coming out. I push with all that is in me. She is here. As I look up, the room is filled with men and women in blue gowns ready for an emergency.

Olivia looks jokingly at them. "It's ok, she already had the baby." Everyone leaves, and I look again at the faithfulness of God, realizing the swelling had just gone away miraculously, and my baby is safely resting on my chest.

Chapter 45
-Foe or Friend-

Gratitude is bubbling over. I look at my new home that God has provided. I see the work my in-laws have done. I love our home. I love my children. My concentration is broken. I hear noises coming from the kitchen. What in the world is that? To my chagrin, I spot it, the chocolate, the feet sticking out in front of the refrigerator. A puddle of chocolate streams its way into the kitchen. A happy Abigail with chocolate covering her entire body from head to toe, and a sneaky Samuel with a bottle in hand.

The image is hilarious. I quickly snap a picture of them. Life in our home is never dull. I never know what will happen in a day. This weekend, I am so thankful to get a little break with my homeschool group. Every week, we get together at my friend Missy's house.

A few of us moms gather and joke around. Our kids play in the huge backyard. And swim in the sweet pool. I sometimes look around and feel so blessed to be a part of this group. I especially love Missy.

I feel I can tell her anything. Just the other day, I was sharing my struggles with the kids and the familiar woes that sometimes happen when homeschooling this many kids. She is always such a good listener.

I feel I can be myself here, mostly. Sometimes, though I fear I am being judged, that is probably just my insecurities. I can trust these ladies. Just let your walls down, I tell myself. We are here to support each other. The meals are so excellent. My other friend Cindy is so kind to me. She feels like a mentor to me.

I feel so comfortable around here. Sometimes, I ask for a snack or something for my kids. Sometimes I just forget things. I forgot to bring towels this time, but Missy is always so accommodating. I wish I could have the gift of hospitality like her, yet sometimes I have a feeling that something isn't right. Am I being paranoid?

Denise is the favorite around here. She is so funny and everybody loves her, but today, though happy, she is sharing the news with everyone. We are having one more baby, guys. The room lights up with joy. I am so excited for her. I just found out I was pregnant too.

We get to have babies around the same time. But is it just me? Do I sense it right? Is there not an excitement for me like there is for her? Stop it, Annetta, I tell myself. I showed up without any food to share this time.

I let Missy know I just brought my own food since I get morning sickness. Missy looks at me with a look. Is that irritation? Maybe that's just me. I can't believe it's been a few weeks since we have all been together at Missy's house. There is a hush in the room. Am I missing something? Denise is smiling yet nervous.

Guys, I have an announcement to make. "We are having twins!" The room erupts into applause. This is so exciting. No one saw this coming. I am happy for Denise. I really am, but where are my twins? I have been waiting since Ryan and I were engaged, and still no sign. It's not just her, but friends from home. Friends from our mobile team. Everywhere, there are announcements of twins. My heart aches for it to be my turn.

Denise is getting help from everyone. People are cleaning her home, bringing meals. Everyone is helping her so much. It makes sense, she is pregnant with twins. But Rachel is only a year old, and I have 4 other kids who are so young. It would be so nice to get help since I have no one to help me. I am completely overwhelmed. My anniversary is coming up, and Cindy has an older daughter; maybe she and her daughter can watch my kids while Ryan and I get away for a couple of days. We haven't ever done anything like this before.

Fear of rejection is creeping up. My heart beats fast. Just call. Just ask. What's the worst thing that can happen? The phone rings. Cindy answers and sweetly asks what I need. I stammer and finally get the words out. "Ryan and I want to go somewhere for our anniversary, and we're wondering if you and your daughter could watch them." Cindy sounds hesitant as her words then came out. "I don't know, let me think about it." I understandably say, "Ok, no pressure, if you can't."

The next day comes, and I ask if they can watch the kids. I give her an out. "If you can't, I understand. "No, if I couldn't do it, I would tell you, she says firmly. "Oh, thank you so much! We can pay you too. I am so happy that I am getting help from someone in the group, even if I have to pay for it, and it gives Ryan and me a break for our anniversary. We prepare everything.

We tell the kids we are leaving on our trip. I feel so loved, so content. The restaurant we stop at is delicious. The bed and breakfast has a beautiful room where we stay. If I could just sleep on this bed and that's it, it will be heavenly. I feel the wind against my face as we venture on a beautiful walk along the beach. The sounds of the waves wash over my weary soul. We find a diner with shells on the wall. An interesting French couple speaks in another booth. Laughter exudes the atmosphere. This is the best anniversary ever. I am reminded of our honeymoon: so much joy and so much love.

It seems as if time is flying by. I think fondly of my trip with Ryan. I am so grateful that Cindy and her daughter helped us. I look at Ryan. "We are going to try for another baby. Am I going to be pregnant again? Without hesitation, he says, "Yes, you will." I am late again. I feel that same feeling. Could I be pregnant? We weren't trying yet, but I think I might be.

Yes! Again, joy fills my heart. I can't wait to tell my friends! Denise is big now and ready for these babies. I scan the room and tell them. I am pregnant now, too. Joy is in the air. They are happy for me. Ding dong. Who is that, I wonder? Missy leaves a bag of groceries and a massive box of goldfish. That girl is so kind. She really loves me. How did I get such a good friend? I like when we go on lunch dates and can share about homeschool curriculum, testing, or whatever is on our minds.

My next appointment is already here. These scans always make me so nervous. You are measuring big, but it's probably because this is baby number six! All my tests are negative for gestational diabetes or any other health conditions. The phone rings, Annetta, we are throwing you a baby shower and wondering what day works. My mind is spinning. My heart is overcome with love. I just need to let my walls down and truly trust these ladies.

The restaurant is beautiful. Smiling faces are greeting me. We want to celebrate you and your Rebecca. The room sparkles with laughter and love. I see the gifts, the cake, and feel so much love. I have truly found my tribe, and I am so thankful.

I am excited to get my water birth finally. The worship music fills the room. The tub is being filled. I can imagine slipping into the blissful tub to take the edge off. As I enter in, the cares of the world fade away. It's only me and Jesus. The rest of the world fades away. Suddenly, I need to push. The team jumps in and panics. "Get her out of the tub now!" Panicked voices try to remain calm. "Annetta, look at me," my midwife says. "You can do this, and you need to do this." I push standing up. The baby is stuck. My midwife calls for help. They come over and yank and yank as I am pushing the baby out. I don't feel I am in my body anymore. The midwife put her on the floor. She yells, "Well, pick her up." I am placed on the bed and feel forgotten about as Rebecca is moved to the heating bed. There is so much energy in the room.

"Oh my gosh, she is so big!" It's like a paparazzi in here. Pictures are flashed as I am sitting alone with the placenta still in. "Sorry, I just have to look at her." She is almost 11 lbs. This is the biggest baby we have ever delivered in the midwifery building. She got stuck, not at her shoulders but at her stomach! She is one big baby.

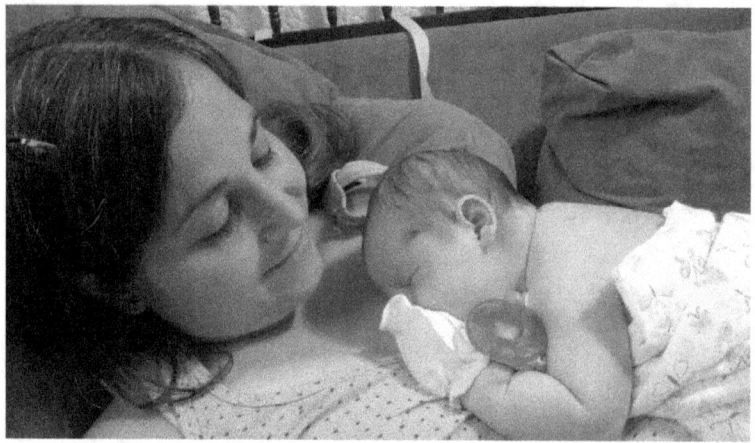

Miraculously, I didn't tear. God blessed my body yet again. They place her on my stomach, and I instantly fall in love with her. She is my big, beautiful baby and came out fast. My delivery was only about one hour long.

Meals appear, and I am so thankful. Life is exhilarating. I check my emails. That's curious. One from Missy. I open it. The words begin to swirl as I read each sentence. A pit forms in my stomach as the reality of what I read catches me off guard. Never would I have expected this from her. She is my friend. The tears stream down my face as I continue, "You are too needy. You have asked too much. You borrowed my towels. You didn't bring food to events."

My face burns with rejection. And one last final point. "You asked Cindy to watch your kids, and it was too much; she never wanted to do it." You are too much is the lie that twists like a knife in my heart even deeper. She writes bible verses, maybe to ease her conscience. What does the last line say? It couldn't say it... "You are no longer welcome back to our Homeschool group. The decision is final." The pain goes into my innermost being, as the lies of the enemy whisper, "it's been true, you are unwanted and unloved by those closest to you." Pain is now my constant companion, with rejection oozing its venom into my heart.

Chapter 46

-Pain, Pain, Joy-

Everything is cloudy. My mind keeps racing back to that email. That one email that changed everything. I don't want to let anyone in my heart ever again. Darkness is beckoning to go back. Rejection hurts more than any physical pain, they say, and I believe it. Word spreads. Others in the group are confused. Why kick Annetta out of a mom's support group when she needed support? Division strikes like a snake.

The homeschool group begins to crumble. In my hurt, I am not sad that it is falling apart; I feel vindication. Maybe there are consequences for what happened. How do I go from here? I want to stay hidden. I lick my wounds, hoping to find some sort of comfort. The pain won't leave. An old friend reaches out. I replay the story. She listens and prays for me. God uses her to help me see some light. It feels as if she comes down to the tunnel I am in and shines a flashlight in my dark cave.

People call from other groups in the church. God lays it on their hearts to reach out. People begin to pray. The room, my room, is dark and empty. I don't want to get up. Depression is calling me. The lies are louder. You aren't enough. You will never be enough. Nobody likes you.

The words of Missy echo in my head. Beating over and over like a drum. One friend, Melissa, reaches out from the homeschool group. "Annetta, can we talk?" she asks gently. I softly say, "yes." As she comes over, we go upstairs. I don't want the kids to hear. We go into the homeschool room. I peer out of my gated heart at her. Her eyes are tender and soft as she says, "I am so sorry for what Missy did, Annetta. It wasn't right."

Tears stream down her face. I want you to know that I disagreed with the decision to kick you out. There are lots of us who disagree with her. I hear her out. My walls are so big that I can barely hear her talk. She continues speaking with sincerity and love. A piece of my wall falls, and tears begin to fall. I cry deeply as she hugs me. I cry so much I can feel it in the pit of my stomach. When we are done, she hugs me and lets me know if I need anything to call her. She is here for me. God is showing up and helping me through friends.

I continue to recall the conversation. A bitter root is growing like a weed. Someone suggests forgiveness. How can I forgive someone who betrayed me like her? But I knew I needed to forgive. It's been a couple of months, and I knew a face-to-face meeting was necessary. It was risky. It was bold. But I need to be free from this.

Missy and Cindy both agree. We decide on a time and a place. The drive over is heavy and ominous. Anxiety begins to well up in me. My heart beats faster as I approach our meeting spot. "What if it goes worse than before? "What if...what if? The door creaks as I open it. The sky is a beautiful blue. The birds are chirping away. My surroundings do not match my insides.

My feet touch the long sidewalk. I walk for what seems like an eternity. I find a seat in front of the coffee shop. In the distance, a woman approaches me. Is that her? She smiles a nervous grin. "Hi, Annetta." "Hi, Missy. Small talk begins. My insides are twisting with each fake conversation. Is this a mistake? I think to myself. My nerves are wrecked. Missy looks at me and says Cindy will be here soon.

What feels like hours is only minutes as I see Cindy casually walking towards us. She reaches out to hug me. How could she? Small talk again. The elephant in this room is probably the size of a skyscraper. How much longer will we pretend?

Cindy asks if we can pray. I agree because I honestly need Jesus more than ever before. They let me start. My heart feels as if it is bleeding as I make my case. Tears pour out, and Cindy apologizes. I never should have done things the way I did. I recount the conversation we had. I asked you if you were ok. You could have said no. She looks at me, and with compassion in her eyes, says I am so sorry, Annetta. Will you forgive me? Yes, I say with my head nodding quickly. Missy is quiet. "I am sorry you are hurt, but I don't believe I did anything wrong. I still wouldn't let you back in the group." Her words are harsh and direct. How could anyone be so cold-hearted?

I lash out, "Well, I wouldn't want to be a part of your homeschool group again anyway." The gasp fills the air. I cry more. Cindy looks at me and says, "Can I pray? I agree, and the prayers go in. I look up from deep, ugly crying. Cindy says, "Annetta, I think there is more going on than the homeschool group. I think this is only the tip of the iceberg." I say, "It has a lot to do with the homeschool group, though." I say it out loud. "I forgive you both. I feel some of the weight lifted, but words from Cindy almost dismiss the harsh reality of what they did.

It's almost as if what happened, the magnitude of it, was not acknowledged. I feel a little better, but the hurt remains. As I enter the car to leave, I feel God's pleasure for my steps to bring peace to my own heart, but I know it will be a long process to overcome such a deep wound from close friends truly.

Well-meaning friends look at me. "Maybe you will have to be content." I know I have Rebecca, and she is amazing. I love her so much. She is so sweet and loves to cuddle. But Samuel had already said his baby brother is coming. I believe there is another baby. I turn to look at Ryan, in bed, preparing to sleep. "Are we going to have another baby? I ask in earnest. I know we are still believing for another boy. "We will try again, and if it's a boy, great, if not, we will be happy with another girl. We will try one more time.

Time passes, and I think I am a little late. I look, but no, my period is here. My heart sighs. Well, next month we will try again. Weeks pass. And then I am late on my cycle. Maybe this is it. I open the pregnancy test and then take it. The waiting is awful. Minutes feel like hours. Ryan checks the test. With anticipation rising in me, I call out, "What will it say? "Congratulations!" Ryan exclaims. I am so excited. Even in my grief over the homeschool group, I am being blessed.

I finally make it to my first appointment. As we get on the old, familiar rickety elevator, joy begins to fill my heart again. I check in. Everything is good. I lay on the cold, hard table. We are going to take a little peek at the baby. "Wow, how far along are you? I say with confidence, about 7 weeks. I already knew when I missed my period. Oh dear, no, you have here a well-developed baby. You are exiting your first trimester. You are so lucky! I realize I was actually pregnant when I had my full cycle. I feel shock and yet am so thankful. I guess this is going to be an easy pregnancy, I say light-heartedly.

Chapter 47
-Overwhelm, Fear, Surprise-

Everything looks good. Joy fills my heart. But creeping up, I feel a little fear brooding in me. A weird fear. A fear of having high blood pressure. Why did I entertain it? My fear grows. But why? All my other appointments have been great. I decide I can go to the appointment alone. No kids and no Ryan. What could go wrong? The nurse begins to take my blood pressure. I look at her with anxiety in my eyes. "Is everything ok?" Yes, well, your blood pressure is elevated. This time was different. Dixie is our new midwife; I will let you talk to her. I saunter over to her room.

Her eyes glance over me. Without a concern for my feelings, she bluntly says, "The nurse says your blood pressure is high, so we are going to retake it." My heart is pulsing through my chest. I know it will be high, I think to myself, especially now. The cuff is put around my arm snugly.

The noise gets louder. I can feel my heart through the material. The air begins to exhale from the reader. She looks at me and, with concern in her voice, says, "Your blood pressure is very elevated. You will have to go to high-risk and get monitored. "Like right now? I ask sheepishly. "Yes. You can't wait." I am shaking now. The room begins to close in on me. I can't think. "Can I call my husband to come and be with me?"

In almost a mocking voice, she responds, "No, you can't call your husband. If you can't handle this on your own, then how can you handle this pregnancy?" She is rude and lacks compassion. I am rushed upstairs as the anxiety grows. Panic is growing in my heart as I look at the nurse upstairs. "Can I please call my husband to come here?" Of course, she says. "Let's just take a look at your blood pressure. Oh, it is elevated."

"We are just going to leave this on for now," I call Ryan, my voice filled with panic. "Can you please come here? They say my blood pressure is elevated, and I am scared." With a calm in his voice, he says, "I will come as soon as I can, try to relax." Relief is coming.

What feels like hours and multiple readings on the machine all elevated, I think, what is taking Ryan so long? I feel trapped, helpless, and fearful. "Try to calm your mind", the nurse says is trying to be helpful, but nothing is working. Then a familiar voice is heard. Thank goodness it's Ryan. He touches my back and sweetly talks to me. My heart rate begins to drop. My blood pressure returns to normal. The nurse exclaims, "Well, he did it, your husband has the magic touch."

Finally, I am released, but not without consequences. Though joyful and excited for this new baby, the fear of high blood pressure is becoming my focus. Just as I am trying to learn how to cope with the pain of the group, the worry about my blood pressure, my sister calls.

Mom is not doing well again. Dad and Mom are going to need to find a place to live. We need to sell their home and find a place for them to live. My mind is swirling with worry. Not my parents, I think. I try to be helpful to my family while battling all these internal wars.

Day after day, I try to help. I make phone calls. Emotions are at a high. I also buy my own blood pressure cuff to try at home. I become obsessed. It's higher today than yesterday. Ryan is getting tired. He is dealing with it all and trying to support me. I dread every appointment when I have Dixie. She was like a dog after a bone when it came to me and my blood pressure.

Dixie is harsh. She tries to be nice at times, but all I can feel is anxiety when I see her. I try to approach her about an accidental writing from another midwife about me being maternally obese. She tries to say it nicely, but with an abruptness, looks me over and says, "Well, you might be maternally obese. In my heart, I know it is not true, as the other midwife told me it was an accident to put that in there and she could not take it off.

I have only gained twenty pounds, and I know my weight is healthy. Why do I care so much about the opinions of others, yet I do? How could I be obese? My mind is racing as her words hit like darts and says, "Let me be clear, I will not be taking off that you are maternally obese.

Nor will I take off the hypertension, if you come back pregnant, it will say that you have hypertension, and that will never change."

Her fingers seem accusing as these words rattle off her mouth as if she has a personal vendetta against me. She tries to soften the blow. "Maybe this is all maternal hypertension, and it will get better after you have the baby." I feel so out of control, and anger fills my face, and a bitter root worms its way down into me.

Every appointment worry fills my mind. Will I be Ok? I walk into a room. I wait. This time I have Linda. She was so rough with Rachel's birth, but now she is soft towards me. She even tells me how beautiful I am. Maybe she was having an off day back with Rachel. I make my way into the cold, sterile hallway.

The door opens and I lay on my back. Why is my heart racing? I can't calm it down. With wide eyes, she looks at me. Annetta, I can't find the baby's heart rate. Yours is so fast, I just can't tell." Oh no, what if something is wrong? I panic. "She calmly says, let's do another sonogram and see if we can find it." We make our way into the dark room.

My hands are trembling, and we look at the screen. Linda looks calmly at the screen, "Everything looks good. Here is his heart rate. Perfectly normal." Relief fills my body. Now, do you want to know what you are having?" I look up, "I already know we are having a girl. They told us at the last appointment." With a surprize in her voice she exclaims, "No, you are having a boy!"

Disbelief fills my eyes. "Are you sure? Ryan says to look again. "You are definitely having a boy!" Tears of joy slowly fill my eyes. "Are you really sure?" Laughter fills the room. "Yes, you are having a boy." I look at Ryan and with a joyful heart, I say, "we are having a boy." As our eyes meet, we realize how faithful God is. Samuel will be so excited to have his brother.

Chapter 48
-A Rollercoaster-

"You have a choice to make, Dixie says, with all seriousness. Your anxiety is too high. There's something that can help you." Her words are echoing in my mind. "Zoloft." "Oh no, I have taken that before for post-partum depression/anxiety. I don't want to take it," I say with trepidation. "You can think about it and let me know." I don't want to take it. I hate how I feel when I take it. But now everywhere I go, every moment of every day I am obsessing with my blood pressure.

I cannot even get good readings at home. I am processing everything. Could it help me? My new counselor is encouraging me. Maybe it will help you. She knows I have a lot of anxiety and a lot of fear.

I meet with Dixie again. "I don't know if I want to take it. "If you don't take this, Annetta, we will have to make you leave the midwifery center." Is she now threatening me? I look at her with concern in my eyes. "I don't want to be kicked out."

Going against my heart, I agree to take the Zoloft. She approvingly looks at me. "I think this is the right decision and will help you to feel better."

Fear of taking the medicine is overwhelming. I look at Ryan. "What if I have a reaction?" "You will be fine, just take it." I feel his frustration. After all, I am constantly questioning it. He just wants me to get better. The constant panic attacks and fearful episodes are getting to him. I take it. I lay in bed, and I begin to see things. I shut my eyes. It won't go away. Circles and colors fill my mind.

My body does not know how to handle it. I finally fall asleep. I feel strange. I take it now every night. The hallucinations are getting better. I am sleeping, but I don't feel as much. I feel like there's a wall in my emotions. I don't like this, but maybe my blood pressure readings will be better.

I walk in, maybe it will be better this time. The cuff is placed on my arm. The sound is familiar. My body stiffens. My heart begins to race. My blood pressure is still high. I can't fix it, but at least I am still in the midwifery center. I leave discouraged. Maybe things will change later. Blood work is done. I am used to it. It hurts, but I don't look. The vein again is too small. I am used to it using the pediatric needle.

Days pass—the phone rings. Rosie, the other midwife, tries to tell me calmly. "Annetta, I don't want to make you worry, but we got your labs back, and it looks like your blood platelets are very, very low. This is of concern because if they get too low, you can bleed out during delivery." Oh, great, another turn for me.

This one is serious. Dixie looks at me at my next appointment. "Unfortunately, because of your blood platelets, it seems like you will have to leave the midwifery clinic. After all the hoops I jumped through, I still get kicked out. Despair hits me. It was all for nothing. I am getting off this Zoloft as fast as I can. "God, please help me. It's all too much.

Ryan and I pray along with our church. I am told to take chlorophyll, but it's a long shot for it to help. Fear is now my constant companion.

I am tired, and there is so much going on. Do we do it? My heart is torn. Everywhere there is advice. You should know 100 percent if you are supposed to do this. My friends are saying it's time. What is God saying, though? There is some peace there. The Vasectomy. It's so permanent. We have our boy, but what about the twins we have been waiting for? "Maybe we will adopt," Ryan says. I am wrestling with this.

God, if you want us to do this, you have to let me know. I must be sure. I search, pray, read, and seek counsel. But most of all, I have peace. I let Ryan know, and we prepare for his surgery. Walking in the waiting room with my big belly, panic mixed with peace is in me. The day comes. Am I making the right decision? I see it so clearly. I am putting the twins on the altar.

I am giving this to God. My friend Rhonda is on the phone with me. She is talking me down from the panic. "Annetta, stay with me on the phone. He will be ok." Everything will be ok." Ryan walks to the car, almost limping. I can tell he is in pain. He did this for me. He did this for us. We must trust that God has a way of making this work for getting the twins. I will trust God.

Chapter 49
-The Big Day-

It's night. I am trying to rest. What is that? Did my water just break? Ryan hurries to get our things for the hospital. As I slowly make my way down the stairs, I see my in-laws wake excitedly about our news. Peace comes over me as we enter the car. The sky is dark, and yet hope is in the air. The drive is long, yet steady.

I barely make my way in, as a wheelchair rushes to pick me up. The nurses rush to my side to take my blood pressure as we are moved upstairs quickly. "She goes really fast." Her last delivery was an hour. Get her in quick!" Ryan calls all our friends. The church is praying. I am praying. And there it is. A peace that passes all understanding. I remember this. God is here. I sense his presence. It is sweet. It is real.

The nurse looks at my chart. Oh hypertension. I am too tired to correct her. I don't have hypertension. All the nurses and doctors would question why I was high-risk. My blood pressure was fine when I felt calm. I had white coat syndrome, not high blood pressure.

I want to warn the nurse, "I get nervous when my blood pressure is read." She leans over and gently takes it. "How bad is it? I manage to get out. "It's excellent, it's a wonderful reading." Joy fills my heart. Another hour passes. I am doing wonderfully with labor.

The blood pressure cuff is put on. No anxiety. Normal reading. Reading after reading. Normal. I try to relax through each contraction. Breathe. Listen to the music. Soak. "Would you like to take a shower? the nurse asks. The soothing water calms the pain in my body. Linda shows up. Encouraging me to do this. "You are beautiful." Maybe Dixie won't be here today.

The hours continue. I guess it won't be a quick delivery, I quip at the midwife. "It's ok. Just know I must leave, and then someone else will come in."

I lean into Ryan. The nurse tries different positions with me. I am getting closer to meeting my sweet Joshua. Peace again. Joy again. Closer, we are getting closer. The contractions are back-to-back. The nurses begin bringing in blankets and the heater. Ryan looks at me. "You see that, we will meet our baby soon. Suddenly, she comes in. Dixie wants to know how things are. The nurse lets her know I haven't had one high reading." "Dixie looks uncaring. It doesn't faze her. I can't convince her, no one can, that I don't have high blood pressure. It is anxiety caused by her.

"I have to push!" I yell. She looks. No, you can't yet. Dixie pulls me down there to make room. I push and push. It's happening. The baby is coming out. I am almost finished. The baby is out. Suddenly, she reaches up inside of me. It hurts so much. I cry out in pain. She, unfazed by my reaction, moves on. Ryan has an urge to punch her. She gives me a shot down there to help with bleeding, but it might do nothing.

Fear of me bleeding out is on everyone's mind. I am trusting God will protect me, and I am ok. I look at my new little baby, and I am so in love. You deserve this, mama.

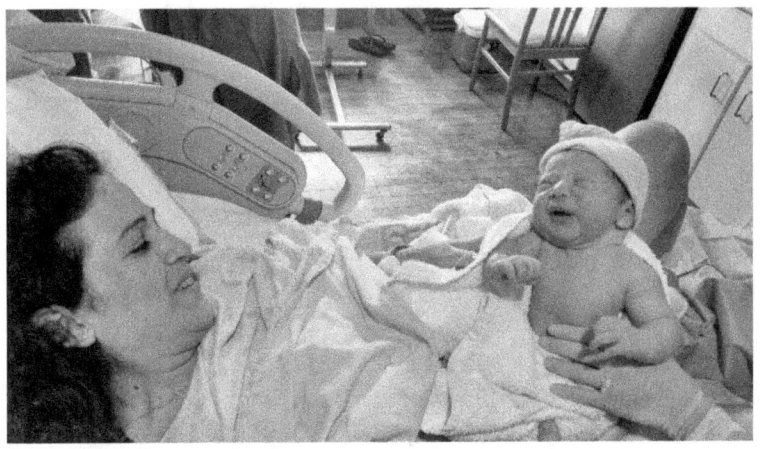

They hand me hot towels and say it's time to relax. "I am so proud of you; the nurse encourages me. Dixie is gone as quickly as she came in. As I am rolled into recovery, the nurses are amazed. I am hardly bleeding. One nurse is cleaning me up. I look up at her. "How are my blood platelets? "Oh, they're fine." I look at her curiously. "I was told they were very low, and I could bleed out." I don't know what happened, but you are hardly bleeding, and you are fine.

I know, God healed me. It was a miracle; how could I not trust God? Peace and Joy fill me once again. God did it. I did it. Love fills me up as I look at my precious baby boy.

Chapter 50

-Space More Space-

Looking out the window, I feel it. I know this isn't our forever home. I am trying to be thankful. I love my little school room. But three bedrooms and seven kids? Five girls in one room and two boys in another. The place is getting tight. I open the curtain. I see our neighbor cooking in their house.

Another day, as I am doing dishes, our neighbor Ricky bops by the window and says hi as he is doing his yard work. My kids go outside to play, and they say it smells funny. What is that? A strong, pungent odor fills the air, as I fear my kids will get high being outside.

Our neighbors' kids are smoking pot. Kids don't go outside in our backyard anymore—the final straw. Weeks have passed. Sweetly watching my kids, I look up. A guy walks to a car window with a bag. Money is shuffled between the two. My mind races to keep up with what I see. The two people think they are sneaky, but I know what they are doing. I find out it was a drug deal in broad daylight. Mama bear is activated.

Praying for the last two years that we would find a new home, I feel we must get out now, especially for the sake of our family.

Every day, I begin praying and talking to Ryan. We need more space. This isn't a good neighborhood. Ryan wants to move, but to where? Everything is out of our budget, but he knows we need to move. We need to look for our forever home, but where would we go? Where would we stay as we look for our forever home? We are too big a family. The desire to move grows in us. I desperately want to move.

That's it. I am going to call and ask if anyone will take our family in if we sell our home. "Sorry, Ma'am, that is just too many people." I panic. I must find someplace. How about this apartment? "You will be a fire hazard." Maybe this house? You must sign a year's contract, or perhaps we can pull off a six-month contract, but we can't commit to anything. Every door is closing. No one wants us. If we sell our home, we must know where we will stay, or we could end up homeless. Suddenly, after praying, I hear that sweet whisper. I know his voice.

An unbelievable thought rushes through my mind. What about an RV? Yes, yes, yes! I am so excited. I approach Ryan. "Absolutely not." We cannot do that. It's too risky. Too expensive. Each excuse is moving this idea further and further away. I approach Jesus again. "Jesus, if you want us to get an RV, please change his heart."

The next day is finally here. I decide to approach Ryan one more time. In my amazement, he looks into my eyes and says, "You know, why not? Let's look into it." My eyes begin to tear up. Thanking Jesus, I know he changed Ryan's mind, and the adventure is now on. Before we list our house, we must get an RV. Our hunt finishes in an exhilarated way. We find the newest and best RV for our family. This one we can use our new van that we got a few months ago. It has bunk beds.

We can put Joshua in his crib right here. Sam can sleep on this pull-out bed. The girls can share bunk beds. And we have the master bed. This is it. This is the RV we will buy. We finance, but that's our only choice. As we pull our RV out, joy fills my entire being.

God once again is faithful to provide. We store it at an amazing RV place.

We have one more question. Where will we live? Every place I call, "You are a fire hazard." You can't have that many people here." Confusion and fear are pulling on me. Did God not say to do this? Another no, panic begins to fill my heart. We have an RV, but nowhere to go. One last place. Ring, ring. He answers. He sounds kind. He is not like the others. As I explain our situation, the answer is to wait. He sounds reserved. But there is a maybe in his voice. "I will call you back and see what we can do." Will he call us back? Will this work out? What feels like hours later, I see the name of his company across my phone. With my heart racing, I answer.

His words hit my gut. "I am so sorry, but that's a lot of people. I don't think we can help you out. I am sorry." Tears begin to fill my eyes. I ask again. "Is there any way you can make this work?

Everyone else is saying no. We are selling our home but need a place in the meantime while we find our forever home. Please help us. Silence. "I want to help you, but let me talk to them again." The worker asks, "Can I call you back?" In between the tears and prayers, I agree that he can call back. Hope begins to rise. Maybe, just maybe, this will work. The phone rings again. "We have decided to help you. You can stay here." My heart swells with joy mixed with amazement that my prayers are being answered. "Thank you, thank you, thank you," as the words rush out of my mouth. "You don't know how much this means to us. Thank you." He gently answers back, "You're welcome, and see you soon."

The house is on the market. We need to sell this home. Person after person declines. Week after week, we clean the home. Someone, please buy our house. Ryan and I pray hard. God, please bring the right family to purchase this home. Let it be a blessing to them and us. Fall is approaching. The selling agent is getting nervous. She knows it's hard to sell a home during the cold season. "Sales drop when we get out of the summer." Finally, good news is approaching. A military family is interested. We make a deal two weeks before Christmas. I ponder God's faithfulness. I am amazed. He is working all things out.

We pile our stuff in a nice storage place. And get our RV. It is New Year's Eve as we drive to our spot in the amazing campground. God comes through, and there is joy in our family. It begins to snow, and in amazement, I look up, full of gratitude that once again God came through.

Chapter 51
-Joy, Joy Freedom-

Every day is so sweet. "Can I please go, Mom? Another event, another day in paradise. The pie-eating contest is so fun. My kids' eyes sparkle as they win again. Laughter fills the air. Looking around, there is a sense of adventure here. I breathe in the fresh air. No homes next to me. No pot smoke. No danger. Just freedom. Every day I take it in. God's glory. His presence. We are right where we are supposed to be. "Let's go," Ryan exclaims. He and I grab our bikes and ride around the beach. We see a passerby as we ride. What a beautiful day. The sky is open and big. The joy I feel is deep. God is so good to us.

I do our school with the kids, then it is off to more play time. Every day we are still looking for our dream home, but the wait is glorious. I pick up a broom and clean. Thirty minutes pass, and the whole RV is clean. I can get used to this. Still, the space is tight.

Laundry must be done daily to survive, and so we know we cannot stay here forever. However good it is, we remind ourselves, it is only temporary.

We call the agent. We know what we want. We want our forever home. We want land and a house, not connected to any other houses. We want a house that is big enough to handle our family size. "I do have a house in mind. We only have a small price to work with. We are hoping for a house in the 200,000 range with land and a big house. The previous agent said there is nothing like that. At least our new agent has faith and, though somewhat skeptical, he offers to help us. We find a house in Pungo with 5 acres. My heart begins to soar. Maybe this is it.

The house is small with a different, older smell, but I justify that away since there are five acres of land. The land is long and wide. I can see myself here. Almost caught up in my thoughts, the dogs begin to bark. A neighbor approaches us. "I think it would be great if you moved here. Just letting you know, though, the previous owner said I can let my dogs roam back here and have a spot just for them". "Oh, okay, we politely say," but inwardly, I am not okay sharing the land.

The price is higher than we want to pay, but it is five acres! The peace is not here. Back and forth we go. This could be it. Do we compromise? With reluctance, we decide to keep looking for our dream house. Our agent looks impatient, yet expectant. Yes, that is a crazy thing to find, but I will be praying for you guys, too."

My mind reminisces over the house that had 5 acres on Sunray Avenue. It is on Sunray Avenue. I remember looking at it longingly through the window, praying that Jesus would let us have this house. It says it is up for auction, but then quickly says it is not for sale. The roller coaster is up and down. We can't ever get in it. My father-in-law kindly takes me to the courthouse to see if we can bid on it. With anticipation, we walk to the courthouse and see it has been cancelled. The house that could be our dream house is out of our reach. In the meantime, we continue looking at other homes.

This house might be it. It has some land like what you were looking for. A giant snakeskin greets us as we walk towards the front door. The house is small and old. The door creaks as we open it. There is nothing there. This will take lots of work. The agent looks at us with a remorseful look. "Hey guys, I think we can do better." I am so thankful we have an agent looking after us. This next house is great, he says with a perk in his voice.

We approach the house. We quickly realize the owner lives next to this house and is watching from a distance. "That's weird", Ryan says with a disdainful look. "Why would the owner be on the same property?" I feel the same way, though, trying to sound excited too. The house is ok, but nothing exceptional. The horse in the back looks curiously at me and the kids. "Now that is so cool to have a horse in the backyard, maybe we could ride it sometimes." We could afford it, but is this really our home? The agent asks if we would be willing to take this house, with evident frustration in his voice. We call him in the evening. "So sorry, this is not the house." Back to the drawing board. It feels as if every house, everything is a no. There is no peace, and there is no door opening for us. We continue to pray.

Though we love the RV park, there is a fire in me to find a new home. Every night we search. Maybe a new one will pop up. Then the agent calls. I think I found something that can work. The house is on two and a half acres of land. It is close to Ryan's work. We make the drive. The house is small, but we can renovate it. Maybe add a second floor to it. We begin to dream. We can add ziplines across the yard. I can see myself here.

The only issue is that the house is unique. Our room is so small that we couldn't fit a bed and a dresser in it. The asking price is 165,000. Then we can get a loan and renovate it. I pray, "God, please let us have this house. It can be my dream home.

The battle begins. The owner leaves the country. Things get difficult. I find someone who can build for us. But everyone says, "Maybe there's something better." Patience is wearing thin. The RV, though glorious, is losing its appeal. I can make this happen. I call people. I am overly persistent with the agent. I call over and over. I must make this work. Nothing is falling into place. People begin to talk. They quietly approach me. "Maybe you need to compromise a little bit.

Maybe you don't get the land." No, I believe God has something for us. But now I am obsessed.

I find a sweet place to pray by my RV. I have no other choice. I come boldly to God. The trees are moving with the wind. The sky is brightly shining through the leaves. I find a little place to cry out to Jesus vulnerably. In the middle of my rant, I hear softly, "Watch, wait, and see what I am going to do." Without pausing, I assume that the house I am looking at is going to be ours. That's it. I just need to keep pushing and believing.

I show up at church the following weekend. My eyes are weary from the waiting. How much longer, Lord? I make my way up to the front. I approach the calm prayer leaders. I confess, I want this house. She looks at me and, with sternness, covered in love, says in all seriousness, "This is an idol in your life." My eyes fill with tears. I softly respond, "I guess I need to repent." "Yes, you do," she says with a firmness in her voice. I drop to my knees and repent.

God forgive me, I say in a sorrowful voice. Please help me. I surrender the house to you." As I get up, I feel different. I don't know what will happen, but I will trust Jesus. The following week, again, this time with humility, I come to the front at church.

This time, the prayer lady looks at me tenderly. "I have a vision. I see a house with so much land. I see trees everywhere. God is going to do it." I cry. I know it's him. I feel it in my heart. He wants me to put him first and then trust that he will give me the desires of my heart. He loves me, but he wants it to be in his time. This time, I wait in hopeful anticipation. I know God is speaking to me and will do what he says he will do.

It is nighttime again. The kids are occupied. It's our routine. We look at houses. This house is enormous. It has two acres of land, and it's down the road from the one we are trying so hard to get. 250,000. Ryan looks at me, and with a solid no, he says, "We can never afford that." I know the house is so much nicer, and I secretly think it is too good a home for us.

It is beautiful, and we would not have to build a second floor. A boldness comes over me. I call the agent with a giddiness in my voice, "I found a house down the road." Can you see if they will come down for us? I look at Ryan with daring eyes. I take the plunge. "Can you ask if they can go down 25,000? The agent's voice chokes. Well, I guess I can do that. I mean, what will it hurt? They can just say no. Within minutes, he calls back.

His voice is loud with excitement! I can't believe it, they said YES!!! Ryan looks at me, shocked as well. The agent says, "Let me make sure and ask some more questions." The ball begins to roll. We come to look at it. My children love this house more than any other house. As they go up and down the stairs, they all exclaim, "This is the house!" We look at all the appliances and carefully inspect the house. Then we look outside.

We know this is it. This is the house for us. Before we know it, the papers are being signed. I look around, blown away by the faithfulness of God. His plan is so much better than mine. I was demanding all the other ones, when he had the best in mine. Friends, come and help us paint. We get help moving into our new home.

After all is said and done, I look out at our big, beautiful yard, and I hear the Lord say, "Hold onto what I did here; you will need it for the babies." I knew he was talking about the twins. What a funny thing to say. I tuck it deep in my heart, knowing I will need it later. For now, I bask in the answered prayer, the fulfilled vision he gave.

Chapter 52
-Stepping Out and Dancing-

My feet and hands are shaking. Really, God? Is that you? Years ago, he asked me to run in an unknown church on mobile teams. I was scared but obeyed, and when I did, a lady came running to me crying. She says through tears in her eyes, "I just asked God to help me dance like David, and then I saw you. You confirmed to me what I was to do. Thank you so much for obeying him. My heart was overcome with gratitude.

Why am I so scared to obey this time? I know his voice. The moment passes. Regret fills my heart. Why didn't I obey him? I approach others. To my surprise, God had also asked them to run. "Wait, God told you to run, too? Why didn't anyone do it? I make my way home, still remorseful that I didn't obey him. I think to myself, God, it doesn't matter what anyone thinks; if you give me another chance, I will do it. I would rather sleep in peace, obeying you than men.

The following week, the feeling is stronger. I hear it, run. My heart beats faster. I look fearfully around me. Oh God, I hope this is you. My feet feel like cement. The fear of what others think consumes me. I move my feet one after the other. Before I know it, I head towards the front. I continue running. My feet feel lighter. I make it all the way around. Something is breaking in me. I make it back to my seat. I feel it in my heart. "Well done, faithful servant." I catch my breath.

Ryan looks at me, "Feel better?" The look of a proud husband fills his grin as I tenderly look at him. Hoping it was one and done, God asks me to do it again. Each time I do it, a little bit of fear falls from my heart, going beyond the walls I built around myself.

I see it. A vision. It has been building over the years. The Lord speaks to me. "You will be my Moses to set my people free in dance." I see banners. I see streamers. I see free movement. Nothing is holding them back. It's a David dance. It's a David freedom. My heart begins to burn. I want it for me. I want it for them. As William Wallace rode onto the field, face painted blue and white, eyes burning in his eyes, I identify with him. Freedom! Freedom! I want others to dance freely. The freer I get with dancing and running, the bigger my heart gets for those around me to experience this.

I want to know and learn more. I attend a spiritual warfare dance class. Yes! We are doing more than just moving our feet. God calls us out to be the first ones in the war. Braveheart Freedom Dancers. The battle is fierce, but God is bigger. I want to dance in the back, so that I won't be a distraction, I tell Jesus. "No, go to the front." I hear the Holy Spirit say. I know I must obey. But I pray, "let me not be a distraction."

My hands go up. I see my Jesus. Audience of one. I learned that in SOPA. As my feet begin to move, I just start turning. I start dancing, freely.

I am at church, dancing away, when an old friend comes to me. She is carrying something. What is that, I wonder? In a serious tone, "God told me to buy this for you." I want to invest in your gift." It is a beautiful banner, with a big, beautiful lion and soft colors. I stammer, "Thank you so much." She seriously looks at me, "You are welcome, just remember to dance for him." Gratitude hits me. God is speaking to me through others. My heart continues to grow. Again, a passing thought, a whisper.

That sweet voice of the Holy Spirit. Buy streamers and buy banners. I must obey. I bring them to church, and God surprises me. "See that little girl, give one to her." Suddenly, I am passing out the streamers to children one at a time. At first, only a couple. Some agree to come to the front and dance. Some decline. But it's my job to be obedient. Every week, I begin handing them out. Sometimes fearfully and sometimes with joy on my face. Every week, a couple more kids would join me at the front. I begin inviting adults.

Slowly, more and more people show up at the front. I keep bringing more banners, more streamers. This Sunday is different, though. I see adults and children come forward. The music is flowing. I open my eyes. The Lord reminds me of the vision and the word. Banners of all different colors are waving. Dancers are abandoning themselves in worship. Joy fills the air. His word echoes deep in my soul, "You will be a Moses to them and set my people free."

Chapter 53
-In the Waiting, God is Healing-

I am willing to lay it down. I am ready to grieve. The pain deep in my heart comes. I try to come up for air. My prayers are dark and heavy. "God, I am ready to grieve. I don't see how we will get these twins. Maybe it will be an adoption. But I am sad. I am sad I will never be pregnant again. Never feel the baby kick in my body again. Never experience the elation after the baby is first born.

Friends around me are pregnant again. Longing. I am longing for it. Tears stream down my face. I feel a loss of not being pregnant anymore. I see the door is shut. I am praying. Maybe it's time to move on. I need to go inside. I make the long and heavy walk upstairs. Alone, I cry deeply. Grief is like a sharp arrow in me.

I hear the words of well-meaning friends. Grieve and move on. You have other children to care for. But I know there's more. I know what God spoke. But it must be adoption. I hear it, it's a gentle whisper. I hear a question go through my mind. "Why are you weeping? Don't grieve. Do you believe I can do the impossible?"

God, is that you? It's almost as if I can't grieve. There is a hope that I can wait. Could it be? Could I get pregnant again? Logic fights faith. Ryan had a vasectomy, and unless he gets a reversal, it is not possible. My steps down the stairs are slow. I approach Ryan, and as I tell him that maybe we can get pregnant again, his answer is hard, harsh. His answer is no. No reversal. His face becomes irritated. He thought everything was finished. We both prayed and felt God tell us to get the vasectomy. He had a vasectomy, so he thought we were adopting.

"You are not getting pregnant again. When we did not have the twins naturally, I believed we would adopt, but that is it." There is a finality in his voice. Anger rises in me. "Why stand against what God is doing?" I question.

I pray and wait. Frustration enters our marriage. The wait is getting hard. I pray once again, God, if this is from you, please change Ryan's heart. Ryan begins to pray. His heart softens to me and Jesus as we both want to know God's will. We both start praying for confirmation about the pregnancy. Hardly anyone knows what we are waiting for. When Ryan's surgery happened, there was a sense of finality, and I wrestled with how God's promise of twins would come to pass. Our friend Barb, who works with an adoption agency, is coming to Virginia.

My heart is ready to hear, yet I'm nervous about what will happen. Something strange happens; Barb does not encourage me to adopt when she hears about our waiting for more babies. Instead, she encourages me and prays for a miraculous pregnancy. She could easily promote her agency. Why is nothing happening? Ryan is praying and asking God to speak to him.

He does not feel we are to adopt now. Snowflakes? What's that, I ask curiously. "It's the babies that are usually left over after IVF treatments. Instead of throwing them away, you can adopt them." Ryan is doing his research.

With an open mind, I investigate it. Snowflakes are expensive, but maybe we can make it work. The longer I search, the less peace I feel. Ryan feels the same way. But adoption appears to be going away, too. "Ryan, you need to get a reversal, I say, trying to take things into my own hands. Aggressively, I question our decision to do the vasectomy since what I heard from Jesus recently changed everything.

My face also breaks out in strange acne. It begins to grow on my face. I don't know what it is. I use all I can. Panic arises in me. Every day, I am hoping it is gone. Tea tree oil does nothing. I cover my face in shame every day. I hate pictures of myself now. I try to cover my face in makeup, and nothing helps. It only grows. I cover my face with my hair to hide the hideous growth now forming on both sides of my face.

Finally, I went to the dermatologist. I walk in, head facing down. As the doctor approaches me, he tries to hide his reaction. "Looks like your phone, or upon further investigation, it looks like hormonal acne. The only way that it can go away is with birth control meds. "But we are still trying to get pregnant," I say with hesitancy in my voice. He hands me a different type of medicine to help; I take it with me, but refuse to use it. God, are you punishing me? I ask accusingly. Now I have an awful thing on my face and am waiting to get pregnant again.

I slowly make my way up to pray. Hannah in the bible prayed daily for a child, and the Lord gave her a son. Now I am fervently praying for what I believe is for me. Twins. An unlikely pregnancy. And healing from these painful, large cysts on my face. The service ends. I make my way to the prayer team. I speak to the two women slowly with bated breath. I have tried everything to get rid of my acne except the strong medicine.

I have no peace about taking it. One of the ladies puts oil on my face. She speaks healing over me. Also, they speak to my broken heart. They call me a Hannah from the bible who prayed daily for a son. A peace rushes over me. I am falling but peacefully. I pause for a moment. I try to get up, but I fall back again without them touching me. Ok, Holy Spirit, I will stay. I think I am done. I try to get up again, though weak. I fall back a third time. This time I stay down. One of the prayer ladies speaks to me.

God is saying, "He will do this regarding the pregnancy. Who do you think put the desire in you to begin with?" Another confirmation. My body feels as if a healing oil is making its way through my entire body. "Hormones, line up," they say with boldness. I feel different. I feel lighter. Jesus is helping me. Joy, I feel joy again. The ladies praying look at me and say, "Remember, it might not be instant."

I leave with hope again. Two weeks pass. The abscesses on my face are drying up. I look different. My face is healing. God is truly healing my face. The itchiness is fading. I believe my face is going back to normal. The doctors didn't heal me. Jesus did. Truly thankful, I begin sharing what God has done for me. And in the quiet, I still wait for the pregnancy.

Chapter 54
-Failed Dreams-

Becky, one of my best friends, prays for me. "I know you're going back and forth with all of this, regarding being pregnant; I see you, Sarah, who is 13, driving a big white van, and there are these kids, and I see two car seats. You were telling Rebecca and Joshua to be careful with the babies, but Sarah was driving." My heart is confused. I thought I might be pregnant now. It has been months since the word was given.

My cycle is late. My belly appears bigger. Nauseousness is appearing. I think this can be it. Right now. Why give me a prophecy for something years from now? Ryan is praying and feeling God show him I will have a supernatural pregnancy also. We both get a beautiful song that is about faith that happens to play when we are both in front of the church. This right now. This can be it. Am I pregnant? We don't take a test. But we still do not know.

Ryan looks at me. I look at him. "I think I might be pregnant, Ryan." "I think you might be too; he says with a loving tone in his voice." As we go on this beautiful walk, my face is beaming. The family is running all around. I look at the glassy pond reflecting off the golden sun. Peace is in me. My face is perfectly clear now. Life is so good.

I feel fresh, I feel light. I go to the bathroom. What do I see? Is that blood? Bright red blood? I call Ryan in a panic. Ryan, I moan out the words. I am bleeding. Are you sure? Yes, I say. Please come home. I feel as if all my air is leaving my body. The blood increases. There is so much blood. He comes home and greets me with sadness like no other. Just this morning, he was going to write a pregnancy announcement. We have been praying daily for the promise, for the pregnancy. He cries. I cry.

He holds me. I can't handle it anymore. I escape his embrace and run to the RV. The pain is so deep I can barely move. Why God, why? I thought I was pregnant. But I am not. Knives of betrayal cut through my heart. "God, this hurts so bad." How can I trust you right now? Ryan enters the RV. He hugs me. He holds me. "Please give me some answers", I say in desperation. "I don't have any, he solemnly confesses.

Hurt is in his eyes. Confusion at his core. We both must decide, in this hurt, in this mess, that we must still follow Jesus. My friend advises me, "Annetta, you must go back to Jesus and find out if you know that you know that this is from him. And you get that confirmation from him and not a man."

The next day, I walk by myself. I need to know what God is saying. Please, Jesus, tell me what the truth is. If this isn't from you, please take this away from me. I feel the coolness of the breeze. I feel as if I am to look up. I see my 15-passenger van in the distance. I feel God gently ask me, "Do you remember how long you prayed for that van?

You would look outside and long for the one your neighbor had. Then one day, I provided for you to have one. I provided one for you, even better than the one your neighbor had. And as loud as it could be, I heard, "Trust My Timing." The words began to go deeper than the hurt. Deeper than the loss. Deeper than the confusion. Trust my timing. I repeated it over and over. I got my answer. Yes, this is from God. Yes, it will happen. And it will be in his timing.

CeCe Winan's song is now our song. It is our song for the babies. We even hear it at church when we go up for prayer as a couple. We are constantly praying. I am invited to go up to the front for prayer. A couple that doesn't know what is going on, looks at me and says, "Are you waiting on something, like a promise?" I feel God is saying, I already said 'Yes." Tears flow down my face. I know that is God's voice. Jesus is speaking to me. I give my pain to Jesus over and over. A prayer team from YWAM shows up at church. It is a special event.

The lesson begins with Jarius. He was waiting for God to go and heal his daughter, but on the way, Jesus was stopped by the woman with the issue of blood. The delay is so long that Jarius's daughter dies before they get to her. The delay seems bad. Jarius is disappointed. It didn't happen when it was supposed to. But Jesus's delay wasn't a no, it was just a delay. Jarius still got his miracle. His daughter was still healed; it didn't happen when he wanted it to. I feel as if Jesus is encouraging me to believe. He says to Jarius just like he said to me, "Don't be afraid; just believe." My heart is a little lighter. My faith is a little less broken.

Chapter 55
-Unexpected-

"Annetta, you have to talk to him. Nothing is helping him. I think he is dying." My brother has always been so invincible. I have been fasting for the elections. My mind swirls around government. I don't expect to pray for my brother. My sister lovingly tells me that when you pray, things happen. I am still not used to my sister calling and asking for prayer.

My sister has been calling me for the last several years with prayer requests. "Things happen when you pray, she would say affectionately. Now here's a prayer request that is bigger than all the other ones. I have been praying for my brother for many years. "Ok, yes, I will do it." We set it up. It is just me and him.

He had taken medicine from a friend that was only meant to be taken for a couple of weeks. He had been on it for around eight months. His body was breaking. His nerves were dying. He couldn't get off the floor. His family had left. "There's only one thing that can help; I tell him with compassion in my voice. He thinks he is going to die.

I feel the spiritual battle before me. Not today, Satan. A boldness comes over me. "Jesus is the only one who can help you, " he says, fighting it. I don't think my Jesus is the same as your Jesus. "There is only one Jesus," I tell him frankly. We talk. It feels like hours have gone by.

He will call me tomorrow. My husband and I pray. My friends pray. The church prays. The messages go off. The next day comes quickly. As if a tug of war is happening, I tell him again that I will pray. The prayers are helping. Something is happening. I ask, "Are you ready? Are you ready to pray and accept Jesus?" To my surprise, his voice weak with sickness, says, "Yes." Excitement fills my heart. "Ok, pray with me, "Jesus, please forgive me for everything I have ever done wrong.

I believe that you died on the cross for me and rose three days later. I ask that you come and live in my heart. Amen." His words match mine. He repeats it word for word. "Amen." The depth of joy I feel supersedes everything else. I pray healing over his body. He feels things begin to shift in his body, and he begins to feel better. I know my brother is now going to heaven.

I share the good news with Ryan and my in-laws. Heaven is rejoicing. My brother, who ran from God most of his life, has now accepted God. What a fantastic, beautiful day. The days go on, and in each conversation, he sounds better. He begins to heal. Thank you, Jesus, for this answered prayer.

I hear it. I feel it. "You need to tell your dad the gospel right now." I feel the Holy Spirit speaks to me. I have been talking to him, but I feel an urgency. My sister has been saying that he is really struggling. He sounds anxious. I know I must call him. My heart feels as if it is burning. He answers the phone in a cheery voice. "Annetta, thanks for calling!" "How's the weather over there? It's good, Dad. I need to talk to you about something.

My voice is intense. I feel I am on a mission. Dad, are you a Christian? "His voice is uncomfortable. "Well, I told you I have gone to church." Ever since my wedding, he has been more open to church, but nothing came of it. I ask boldly, yet lovingly, "But have you accepted Jesus? It's more than going to church." The words become serious. I feel Jesus's longing for my dad to accept him. "Dad," I say passionately, "Jesus is the only one who can help you." The words hit him directly. "Do you want a second chance? Like to be forgiven for everything you have ever done?

Are you ready to accept him?" His voice steady and firm on the phone, "Yes," he says. I am shocked by what I hear on the other end of the phone. "Then let's do it." I ask him to repeat after me, "Jesus, I believe you died on the cross for me, rose three days later. I ask that you forgive me for everything I have ever done. I ask that you come and live in my heart." As he repeats the words after me, a joy so deep enters my heart. I feel the power of the words. With excitement in my voice, I exclaim, "Dad, everything you have ever done is forgiven. You have a clean slate!" Now I know my dad will be in heaven one day! He gently says, "Annetta, I am so proud of you. I really am."

My heart feels healed, going so deep. My dad is proud of me. But it isn't only he who is proud of me; I feel Jesus is so proud of me. I never thought life could be this good. Tonight, I will sleep well.

I share with everyone what has just happened. So many are rejoicing with me. Maybe I can have a new relationship with my dad. Hope is on the horizon. A new call comes in. I wonder why my sister is calling. Dad has been fighting against getting the COVID-19 vaccine. The place he is at wants him to get it." "Well, can't he say no? I ask suspiciously. No, they want everyone to get it. Anger begins to arise. I don't understand why everyone is being made to get this shot. I have no peace about that thing. He gave in once with the first shot, and now they want him to get another one? My dad is scared. He doesn't want to get it, but they are giving him no choice. He takes it. And everything changes.

My sister calls with panic in her voice, Dad is not doing well. They gave him the vaccine, and he is going downhill. Maybe he will get better. Days pass. He is not getting better.

He has been admitted to the hospital. Why is this happening? God, please help him, I pray. But nothing is working. Bible camp is a good distraction. I continue to focus on the kids, but I feel uneasy. My sister calls, "Annetta, Dad is really sick. I don't know how long he has." The world begins to spin. I can't think straight. I start to sob. I find my friend Margie. The words come out of my mouth in a surreal way. "My dad is sick. I don't think he is going to make it." "Well, go. We got it here, and we can take care of your kids."

I find the owner of the camp, and in hysterics, I let her know what is happening. "You are free to go. It's ok. Everything will be ok." She knows about me leading my dad to Jesus. She celebrated with me. I call my husband. I can hardly breathe. How do I handle this? I must leave. I drive the car slowly and in disbelief of what is happening. Somehow, as plans unfold, we still go to Busch Gardens that night. I am in a daze.

My husband asks again. Annetta, do you want to buy the plane ticket? I see a fork in the road. I know I should go, but I am so scared of flying, and I would have to fly by myself. I am shaking. I look at Ryan, and as everything is in slow motion, I look around and softly, fearfully, I say, "Yes, buy the plane ticket." Before reality hits, I hear, "Done." I bought the ticket.

Chapter 56
-Beauty from Ashes-

It's a whirlwind of events. I am leaving the next day. In between crying, we arrive at the airport. Many are praying for me and my family. And a thought hits me; I am so grateful I led my dad to Jesus before all this happened. I remember God said he needed to know now, with an urgency. My dad accepted Jesus in June, and now it's August. The fear is taking my breath away. I look at Ryan, "I can't do this." In a calm voice, he answers, "Yes, you can. You are going to be ok. God is with you." We walk as far as we can together.

The loud sounds of the airport are buzzing all around. I look back; he is gone. I am alone. My dad might be dying. Panic lurks its ugly head once again. My face flushes as I go through security. The lady looks at me, and uncontrollable sobs pour out of my body. Everyone, including me, has a mask on. "I know I am not supposed to do this, but can I give you a hug?" I nod my head.

The hug brings temporary relief, but it's as if I am not alone. I am being carried. I find my seat. My heart is heavy with grief and the unknown. I have my mask under my nose, just like another passenger. The flight attendant abruptly jolts towards them, reprimanding their usage of the mask. I hope they don't yell at me, I think to myself. The same attendant comes to me. Softly, compassionately, asking if I need anything. "Let me know if I can get you anything," he says with a reassuring tone. God is using people to cover me. Love me. Even strangers. Finally, the first plane lands. Now, round two, I am better, but I can't wait to get off this plane. It lands. A sliver of joy hits me. I survived the plane ride.

As I get my bags, my sister greets me. It's been years since I have seen her. Though we hug, we both know this is not a happy trip. We will visit Dad tomorrow. The doctors have moved him. He is not doing well. I am so excited to see my sister, but I am not happy about my dad. My dad has always been the healthy one. He is not supposed to be sicker than my mom. As we arrive at the house, I do not know what the future will hold, but I know God brought me here, facing all of my biggest fears again.

He will help me. We arrive at the hospital. The lady's directions sound muffled and slow. The gowns are placed on, the masks, and the extra shield. Remember always to keep this on. The long walk to the COVID hall is frightening, but I hear this in my head, "Though I walk through the valley of the shadow of death, I will fear no evil." Over and over, it is playing like a soundtrack in my head. The words comfort me, even strengthen me.

The sterile hallways try to pull me into anxiety. The nurses lead us. Your dad is in here. The heavy door is open. The room is dimly lit. My dad lies on the hospital bed, weak, unmoving. He has machines connected to him, but his face is still normal. Claustrophobia gets to me. My dad can't be this sick. I must get out of here. I exit the door. I try to compose myself. My sister quickly comes out. "Annetta, I need you. You must come back in." I can't. It is too much."

Annetta, I have to call our brother, and I cannot without your help." I look at her and know I must go back in. I feebly nod my head. I come beside my dad. "Hello Annetta", he weakly speaks. "Hi, Dad. How are you, I uncomfortably ask. I am ok. "Can I pray for you?" The words softly come out as I pray for his comfort, for his peace and healing, although I already feel God has told me he is dying and won't make it. We brought in a CD player with my dad's favorite artist, Neil Diamond. Sweet Caroline begins to play.

I feel I am caught up in a dream. We joke about bringing his favorite music in. Everything is emotional. My dad, my dad is dying. I reach my brother, whom I had led to Jesus in December, on the phone. He is still in the Czech Republic. They chat. My brother tries to comfort him. The moments pass quickly yet slowly.

"We will come back to visit you, Dad", my sister says. "I love you, Dad", I say, not sure if I will see him again. I hear him say, "I love you too." We go outside the room. I feel so bonded to my sister and my dad. This changes everything. I shiver at the thought of not getting on that airplane out of fear. We go outside and spray ourselves down with as much Lysol as possible, after all, the COVID unit is a scary place.

After we arrive at the hotel, I walk down the fancy halls and find a quiet place to call my friend Veronica. She is there for me so much. I tell her I believe God has shown me my dad is going to die. She feels the same but encourages me to be present and keep praying. She lets me know I am not alone, and the church is praying for me. When I return upstairs, I hide myself in the bathroom tub and begin crying hysterically. "God, this is too much, I can't do this," I call my friend Chrissy.

She lets me know it is going to be ok. She prays for comfort and peace. I don't know what I would do without her and Chrissy. I call Ryan to let him know how things are going. He is my rock and support. I am so thankful he is constantly there for me.

My dad is getting worse. Every day, we are running around, talking to new doctors about different treatments. Nothing helps. My other brother is on his way from California. He knows he needs to see my dad quickly. We just don't know what will happen. My dad is moved to another unit. This one has the room around him. My brother from California is on his way. It's only been two days, and I am so grateful I got there when I did. My other brother is on his way from Europe. Time is ticking.

As if a joy bubble is dropped into the mix, my sister, brother, and I go to the mall. My sister, in her sneaky way, says we should all get on the robotic driving animals—a mischievous grin forms on my face. We tell my brother he must ride them. Laughter fills our hearts as all three of us adults ride along the mall, pointing at each other and taking pictures. My brother looks mortified but happy. Thankful for a slight reprieve, we head back to the hotel. My brother can see my dad.

We wait and get bad reports from the doctors. They won't give him the medicine that we want them to. The doctor insists on a do-not-resuscitate order. His lungs are like a solid mass. It's inhumane not to have a DNR. We insist, and the time creeps by. Why is he not getting better? My other brother, who was traveling in Europe, was almost here. Please let my dad make it long enough for him to say goodbye. It is too late.

They will not let my brother see my dad. The Lord had already told me he was not going to make it when I got there, so every step almost seemed fruitless, knowing he did not have long.

Almost everyone is here. We all begin to reminisce. Laughter fills the room. We are constantly talking with my brother from the Czech Republic—the phone rings. My sister answers with concern in her eyes. The phone is put on speaker. We all listen intently as she shares about my dad. I am so sorry, we tried to bring him back, but we couldn't. Again, I am so sorry. Tears fill my sister's eyes. I can't breathe. I run to the room and close the door. How is this happening? I try to cry. I am numb. A tear begins as I look at the sky. I knew this was coming, but I am not ready. Suddenly, I see something in my mind's eye—a vision of sorts. I see my dad smiling. He is with Jesus. My dad is with Jesus. Joy and sadness mixed envelopes me. Comfort. I feel comforted with a deep pain.

Things go fast. Grief is hitting us all in different ways. What if we had the funeral this weekend? We are already here. Now it will be a whole week since I left for Texas. I look at my sister and brothers, and gratitude fills me up. I am so grateful that I have bonded with them. I am so thankful I said yes to coming by myself. Though I am so appreciative that Ryan is coming for the funeral, the closeness I feel to my siblings is like nothing I have ever felt with them. Ryan arrives, and his hug is nothing short of miraculous. I feel love. I feel at home.

I prepare myself. The day is here. I see the casket, but I don't know if I can go to it. My dad is gone. Reality hits again. This pain is so deep. This pain overcomes me. Sweet Caroline begins to play. His favorite song. Ouch. Next, I can only imagine begins. I can almost see my dad in heaven, full of peace.

He got the second chance I told him about. We are seated in the front. People keep pouring into the sanctuary. Uncles, aunts, cousins. My siblings and I stand up. Each one of us shares a line from a Dr. Seuss book. He always loved Dr. Seuss. He would quote him throughout the day. It is only fitting we read it at his funeral. Sweetness mixed with sadness fills the room. I sit down.

We did it. Relief hits me. I cling to Jesus. God, please help me. Please give me the words to speak. My eyes meet my mom's eyes. She hugs me. I want to help her. I want to comfort her. The preacher loudly announces, "If any of the family wants to share, come forward." My sister goes first. My heart begins to pound. I know I am supposed to go up there. I stand up. I walk towards the front. The church is silent. I make the long walk forward. All eyes are on me. I begin to open my mouth. The words flow out with peace. "My dad always spoiled me. I start to share. He loved taking me places.

Whatever I asked him, he would do it, maybe because he was the baby. Then I knew I had to go there; I scan the room. They need to hear what happened. With a quiver in my voice, I share, "I was talking to my dad two months ago." I knew I had to share. I asked him if he would want to accept Jesus. I shared how Jesus died and rose again, and he accepted it. My dad accepted Jesus into his heart. I led him to Jesus. With passion in my voice, I declare, "I will see my dad in heaven one day." The room exhales. I am shaking as I walk back to my mom. Her hug says it all. She is proud of me. Most of all, I feel that Jesus is proud of me.

My life is forever changed. I can feel it. I hug my brothers and sister goodbye. I have never felt so close to them and to my mom. I love them so much. God has given us a miracle, closeness as a family that we haven't had. I hug my mom tightly. Realization hits me, this might be the last time I see her, as she is old and doing well. I love you, Mom. I will call you soon. I make the long plane trip home, but this time, I am not alone; Ryan is with me.

Mom, Me and my Siblings

Months pass; my sister and I talk all the time. Even my brothers reach out. I must teach at our co-op, and my dad just died. The days are hard. I feel lonely. I feel sad. I feel joy that he is in heaven. I feel overwhelmed. How can I teach at the co-op? Every day is hard. Tears fall and prayers are prayed, "God give me grace. Help me keep going." Christmas is hard. Memories flood my mind. My dad used to decorate with big, beautiful lights. The good things that he did fill my mind. The forgiveness I gave my dad colors my eyes differently. I see the good in my dad, despite the bad. I know that he really loved me, and that makes it so much harder.

As my sister calls, we talk. I remind her of Jesus and how he is helping. The same urgency I had for my dad races through my veins. "You need to share the gospel with her." Boldness once again overtakes me. I tell her that what Dad and my brother had can be yours too. "No, she says, sadly, it is too late for me." Quickly, I retort, "No, it is not too late for you." You can start over right now. Right now, we can pray. I explain to her how I led my brother and Dad. Are you ready to do it? A slight hesitation passes. "Yes, I will do it. I have her repeat the words after me.

Asking Jesus to forgive her for everything. Confessing that Jesus is the Son of God, died on the cross, and rose again. And asking for him to come live in her heart. The moment is powerful. As she finishes, I exclaim, "You will go to heaven when you die, you are saved. I love her so much. I am so happy. I tell Ryan, after all these years, my sister gave her life to Jesus. Shock and joy strike his face. "Seriously?" Yes! Yes! Yes, I exclaim. Peace fills my heart as I ponder this past year. God is so good.

Chapter 57

-Deliverance-

My thoughts are so bad. My friend Nicki is trying to help me. I love chatting with her, her love is evident to everyone around her. She walks me through the pain and rejection I feel. Healing the hurts. Open palms. I know what she means. Let God have it all. Deep tears, deep cries. God is getting me healed a little at a time and using my amazing friends to help. Peace is in my mind and peace is in my heart. I think I am free. Weeks pass. It's gone.

I have been praying with her for what seems like years. But there is still something there. My thoughts. Why are they so bad? I have seen God move. I do counseling. I forgive. Why am I still battling it all?

One of my closest friends, Samantha, tries to encourage me. Our kids have grown up together. We have been best friends for years. She is always there for me. She prays and advises me. She points me back to Jesus. Though she helps me, it only temporarily soothes the raging going on in me.

I feel like Saul from the bible, tormented, and as David plays the harp, peace returns. As all my friends pray and even my counselor, I find a temporary reprieve. I want freedom. Freedom that will last.

Veronica approaches me. She looks at me with a new determination to help me. We have prayed for years, and I always need prayer again and again. Her tone is serious, and her eyes proclaim hope. I know a couple that do deliverance. Maybe it could help you. I have done it, and it was so good." My face is flushed. Fear overtakes me. I don't know about that. The war begins.

I want more freedom, but the fear of the unknown is ominous. "Let me pray about it." The dreams I have get worse. The thoughts grow increasingly evil in my mind. I don't understand how, as a Christian, I can feel this way or think this way. Anxiety, depression, and perversion plague my thoughts and emotions.

I cannot keep living this way. I know things can be better than this. I feel the Holy Spirit leads me back to Veronica. "I want to do this. I can't live like this anymore." I begin the process. I must wait weeks. Why is it getting harder? It feels as if something in me is dreading this meeting. Something in me is dreading it, and it is not me. Tina and Chris set up the appointment. One of my kids gets sick. It feels as if all week, something was trying to stop me from going. With determination in my eyes, I get into the car. Driving is difficult.

I have the urge to turn around. Fear is everywhere. It sounds like something loud. Something screaming. "Don't go!" That's not the sweet whisper of the Holy Spirit. It's an evil feeling. I must get to their house. I don't care, as I ignore the voices in my head. Finally, I see it—the beautiful yard. Trees are moving softly in the wind. I make it. A welcoming woman approaches me. "Hi, I am so glad you made it. I am Tina, so lovely to meet you." Her husband graciously greets me, too. I make it to the couch. Peace is all around me. I am so thankful to be here. Our conversation is calm, superficial.

Then they begin explaining things as they see my obvious nervousness. "You will not get hurt. We will start to ask questions, and if there are things there, we will be casting them out." I knew I had opened the door to witchcraft and knew my dad had been a Muslim. My mom's side had things, but I didn't know what exactly. The sexual and physical abuse I knew had opened doors for the enemy in my life. "How could I possibly have demons if I am a Christian?" My voice was shaky, uncertain.

They calmly and clearly explained, "Your soul can have demons, but not your spirit. Your spirit is born again when you accept Jesus, but you still have a will, emotions, and a soul that is being made new daily. That is the difference between oppression and possession." This is strange, but I know that it is true. We go through verses about deliverance. The room begins to feel closed in, yet I still feel Jesus.

The demons, one by one, are cast out. I shriek. I scream loudly. Witchcraft. That one is big. You need to command this one to leave. I yell, "Get out of me in Jesus' name!" Hours go by. The generational curses and demons are leaving. One is mad that I am still trying to get pregnant. It hisses at me. Satan does not want me or any Christians to have babies. It represents God and his holiness. He finds them repulsive. With all our children we have had and the twins to be, he hates me with a special hatred. The last demon comes out.

My body shakes, and a calmness sets deep in my soul and heart. It's quiet. I feel different. The demons that left have been there since I was super little. Some came in from the sin I committed. Some came in from abuse. Some were generational. But one thing they all had in common. They all had to leave. We finish the session, and peace fills my mind. My mind, which was so tormented before, feels calm. I feel clean. I feel refreshed. I feel new. It's as if Jesus went into the depths of my soul and cleansed me. Suddenly, the price that Jesus paid for me was real. I feel grateful that he would set me free and do it all, even if it was just for me.

Over a year passes, and I am free, but there is one fear that I can't get rid of, the one fear that still plagues me—the fear of flying. My sister calls me. "Hey, Annetta, what would you say to flying out here to Texas so that we can have a happy time together? We will all get together and see Mom." Oh, the plane ride. My words begin to stumble. "Oh, I don't have money for that." She quickly responds, "That's ok, I can pay for your ticket." I am out of excuses. I want to see my family, but I do not want to get on another airplane.

After all, the last plane ride I was on was to see my dad. It's been three years since I last rode on a plane and since I last saw my family. A bubbly yes somehow comes out of my mouth. Plans are made. Though I have been delivered, this fear will not leave.

I call Veronica. My body is shaking with anticipation of my trip. Once again, I must go alone. How can I do this? I can't breathe. My breathing becomes heavy; my heart is beating faster than it has before. "I am coming over," she says with concern in her voice. I talk to her. It's about the loss of control. It's irrational. I can't talk myself out of it. The prayers begin. I repent for partnering with fear. My voice cracks, "I can't do this." The Holy Spirit begins to break through. I must let go. I surrender to Jesus. She casts out fear. She casts out many things. I can't even hear everything. The sobbing continues. Suddenly, I am ok. I look around. I am going to be ok.

Though still nervous, I feel better. Almost free. Ryan brings me to the airport. He prays. I enter. This time, I am not sobbing. This time, I smile. This time I am more confident. I board the plane. My face feels hot. I am flushing. I must go to the bathroom. I feel trapped. What am I doing? I sit back down in my seat. I fumble with my computer, and I know I have the Chosen videos ready to go. I hear the whisper, "Start playing the video."

The plane begins to move. I start the video. The scene begins. The little girl is afraid. Her father, looking at her, says tenderly, "What do we do when we are afraid?" With terrified eyes, she says, "We look to Adonai." I feel as if Jesus turns my face to his. "Look at me. Keep your eyes on me." I do; the video keeps playing. The pilot already says there will be a lot of turbulence today. I hear the Holy Spirit gently say, "Feel that? "It's only air pockets in the sky."

I look outside. The clouds are beautiful. I feel closer to Jesus. I feel ok. Now we begin the descent. "Remember, just air pockets. Everything is fine." Safely, we land. I look out the window of the airport. What do I see? A rainbow just for me. My meal is delicious and filling.

I board the second flight. Again, I hear to play The Chosen. The pilot chimes in, "Sorry, ladies and gentlemen, it is going to be a bumpy ride." Oh great, I think. Really, God? Again, as take-off begins, I turn my thoughts and heart towards Jesus. This isn't so bad. Though bumpy, I am ok. We finally make it to Texas. The Lord is changing me. He is delivering me from my fears. Though my friends pray, only he can truly deliver me. This time, as my sister picks me up, joy is on her face. The whole weekend is filled with laughter and peace, the opposite of what it was last time I came.

Once again, I am grateful fear did not keep me away. I love my sister and brothers so much. My sister drops me off at the airport. The walk begins. As I wait for my plane ride, something different begins. I feel an excitement to get on the plane ride. I think to myself, "I get to ride in the plane," and I knew at that moment everything changed. God truly is delivering me from all my fears.

Chapter 58

-Lemonade, Anyone? -

The hot steaming day influenced Rebecca and Joshua. Today would make a great day to sell lemonade, after all, we just had one yesterday and made some money. Why not today? They move the chairs onto the smooth driveway. "I can't believe it they squeal with delight. $40.00! That is a lot of money. Mom, mom, look at how much money we got! "That's awesome," I call out to them.

Today I am sure will be a busy day. I call Ryan as I sit in my closet and let him know how things are going. Rebecca comes in screaming. "What is going on? He stole it! He stole all our money." She is hysterical with tears. I run outside, my heart pounding and sweat pouring from my hands. Joshua is visibly upset, too. "A man just stole our whole jar!" "Who would steal from kids? Adrenaline rushes through my body.

A pickup is in the distance. "Hey, come back with my kid's money I scream out." They don't hear me. "Mom, that's not the right person!" cries Rebecca. My senses are blurry. Embarrassed, I run outside. "Let's find him", I say. Rachel jumps in the car with me, and Rebecca screams; Mom, don't do this." I ignore her pleas and say sternly, "No, we must find him. As I am dizzy with emotion, a miracle happens. I hear the Holy Spirit say, "Stop, turn around, and call the police. Let me have this and see what I can do." My heart softens. Reality beckons me back.

I call the police. They show up within minutes. All the officers make a plan. "No one messes with children." We give them all the footage we have of the crime. Thankfully, Ryan had a private camera set up. I did the right thing, and now we wait. The officer says maybe the news will reach out. I go for a walk. Jesus, I pray, please let my kids get on the news. I really want something good for them.

I feel it in my heart to let both Joshua and Rebecca know that it is important that we forgive the guy who did this. As Joshua leaves, he responds, I already forgave him, and I am praying he becomes a Christian. Tears fill my eyes as I realize Joshua already knew what to do. My heart lights up in mommy pride.

Ryan posts on the Next-door app. How many people are responding? Oh my gosh, it's going viral. A suggestion for Wavy 10 to call us gets noticed. They call and ask for an interview. I can hardly believe it. God heard my prayers!

Ryan and I ask hesitantly, "Another lemonade stand?" "Yes, we want to do one," Rebecca and Joshua say in excitement. "Let's do it! Let's do it over here with the lemonade stand." We tell Wavy they can share our details for the next stand. Wavy shows up, the kids retell their story, and express forgiveness for what this man did. They capture the hearts of everyone.

The kids let everyone know they are raising money to get a 4-wheeler and a dirt bike, and then to help their sister raise money for missions in Asia. "Come help support these kids as they do another lemonade stand," she says with great joy in her voice.

We think this is it. We got the one interview, now we will wait. The next day, I answer the phone. "Hi, are you Annetta Caldwell, Rebecca and Joshua's mom?" "Yes, I say curiously. I am from Wavy 10, and I would like to come out for a second interview. My heart races. "Yes, I say, when can you come by?" She pauses, "Actually, we are at your door right now." Panic begins. I call the kids outside. The camera comes and we begin again. "This can't be happening," I tell Ryan. We share the story. I wonder how many will come to this lemonade stand.

Another call? Ryan, in utter shock, let me know Inside Edition wants an interview. We prepare the living room. The light must be exactly right. The interviewer comes on. We will begin shortly. The anticipation grows. The questions are asked. "Tell us what happened, Rebecca. She relays what happened, exuberant with confidence. The fear is dissipating from Josh and Becca's eyes. She and Joshua forgive this man. Maybe, just maybe, God is restoring and healing them.

Ryan and I share our hearts. I share my story of having to give this over to God and forgiveness also. The whole thing feels like a dream.

Just when we thought it couldn't get any better, I am scrolling through Facebook, and a message appears. "Hi, just checking if you are Joshua and Rebecca's mom. I was wondering if you would like to bring you and your kids to my studio and share the story about the guy who stole their lemonade stand money. We would love to help find this guy." "Yes, that sounds great," I say enthusiastically.

The morning comes quickly, and with much anticipation, we enter the radio station. Records and pictures are all over the walls. I look in amazement. How did we get here? The radio host approaches us with a gleam in his eye. His friendly demeanor puts us at ease.

The microphones are placed before us. I share one with Joshua, and Rebecca has her own. The kids are natural as he and his co-host banter with the kids. I am sorry this happened to you guys. They both express compassion. We would love you kids to get blessed and raise money for your 4-wheeler and dirt bike. We share our Venmo and Cash App and wait for the blessings to pour in. As we finish, the radio host throws bags of candy to them. Josh's eyes light up. His face says it all; he can get used to this.

As we arrive home, the radio host asks if his friend Jackie can do an interview. Yes, that sounds great. We are preparing again for yet another interview. Jackie is so good with the kids. He even lets me share my part of the story. My words come out effortlessly. I know that is a God thing. A stranger drops by to drop off money. He heard our story. He gets interviewed. Soon, other neighbors are sharing. Is this really happening? We finish and head to my son's soccer game. Someone calls me from Facebook Messenger. "You do not know me, but

I heard about what happened to your kids, and I wanted to get a group of us to come and support them. We are a bunch of bikers from the 757 group." Sure, you can come. That sounds great!" My thoughts begin to wonder just how big this Lemonade Stand is going to be. My husband is delighted. The kids are tired but excited, too. Everyone rushes to prepare for the big day.

Who knows how many will show up or who will show up? My in-laws buy lemonade powder; we have huge containers. I am praying, "Please, God, show up." I ask for his presence to fill the neighborhood. To fill our home and driveway, and for him to get all the glory.

The stage is set. We look. The news is here. Everyone is anticipating this great event. "What's that? My daughter exclaims. We see a group of bicycles coming our way. "Is this where the famous lemonade is? Yes, it is. The kids busily hand out the lemonade.

The money begins to rise in the jars. Our first customers are so generous. There is a buzz in the air. The cars are stopping. One couple gives $100.00 each. There is so much love. So much support. Everywhere we look, blessings, blessings. There is so much, our heads are spinning.

My dear friends Veronica and Nicki stop by. Their eyes grow big as the Ambulances, Fire trucks, and Police officers begin to come in droves. Tears fill my eyes: so much redemption, so much love. The city council begins arriving. They shake our hands. Detectives, sheriffs, all these people. Photos are taken. I can hardly believe it. More radio stations stop by. Then, more news stations. Then we hear them—the roar of the engines. The ground begins to shake.

The motorcycle group appears to have at least 120 riders. Their loud engines drown out all the other noises. How amazing is that? They come to see the kids.

They look at them and ask for the lemonade. 20s, hundreds. The jars fill up, and we bring them in—jar after jar. Money is everywhere. I ask Ryan, "How much money do you think we have?" he whispers, "Thousands."

My dear friend Mayla and her family from down the road have been here helping us all day. One of the motorcycle members takes Rebecca and my other daughter on a ride. Joy fills her heart as she rides down the road full speed ahead.

Who are we to be so blessed? I am reminded once again of God's voice. "Let me take this and I will show you what I can do." I am blown away by God's goodness and faithfulness and the love of the community. As our last customers head out, I know we will never be the same again. 6,500 is counted—so much money, so many blessings. We can get them their 4-wheeler, dirt bike, and give Sarah her money for missions. God is so faithful!

Chapter 59
-But Wait, There's More-

As the day moves on, I hear a knock on the door. My kids say a man is at the door. I come to the door suspiciously. "Hi, my name is Rick West, and I am the Chesapeake Mayor. I am so sorry I couldn't come by yesterday for the big event." I wanted to invite your kids to be presented with an award at our next meeting." My jaw drops. Yes, thank you so much. Here's my card. I will have someone reach out to you. I feel faint.

My kids will be honored in front of the city council. I run inside and tell the kids. I call Ryan. Ryan, guess what? The mayor just stopped by and wants to present an award to the kids at a council meeting. "You are kidding me, Ryan nervously laughs. It's not like we haven't been blessed enough. But God loves to go above and beyond.

News Nation reaches out. We would love to do a live interview with your family. Wow, yes. We prepare our room for the next day. We go on a live news station and share all that has happened.

I get another call and am asked to interview with the New York Times. "It's only me right now," I say timidly. "That's ok, tell us about what happened, and then how the lemonade stand happened. I share the story in detail, and am amazed I am getting opportunities to share, too. They begin pouring in. My kids are tired, but I encourage them to do one more. This one is a radio station from Canada.

I have been praying that CBN would pick up our story, but it has not happened yet. I get another call. It feels like there is something new every day. Hi Annetta, I am from ABC World News, and David Muir is interested in your story and that of your children. We would need a video sent to us right away. I am in shock. I set up the camera in our art room. I share genuinely about what happened. My kids share their hearts. It is short and sweet. I send it off, and to our surprise, it is on The World News. I am blown away. God is doing more than we could ever imagine.

The Virginia Pilot reaches out. Can we do an article on your kids and family? They bring a photographer in. The pictures are taken. We share the details of what happened. And before we know it, the paper runs our story on the front page! How in the world is this happening? I feel as if I am watching a movie. My kids are on the front page of the newspaper?!? How cool is that? I pray for Epoch News to cover my story since they reached out before. They call and ask to do the interview, and my heart is elated when it goes out. It is now going all over China and across the world. God is so good.

Suddenly, what I have been praying for weeks happens. CBN reaches out to us. They come to our house and interview our kids and Ryan and me. Joshua sweetly shares how he chose to forgive the man who stole from him and wanted him to become a Christian. Rebecca shares her heart of forgiveness. Ryan shares his desire for redemption and for the man to get help. I share my side of the story and how I gave it to God, and he changed everything. We taught our kids about forgiveness, but really, it was a lesson for us all.

My heart is full and content. Now we wait for the award ceremony from the mayor. The night was beautiful. My husband, kids, and my in-laws find our nicest clothes. The school board members are so welcoming. The award is presented, lights shine, and pictures are taken. We think this is the last of the Lemonade Stand.

Chesapeake Mayor Rick West

The letter comes in the mail. The Governor sends my kids a hand-drawn letter commending them and their parents. What an honor. We see God's favor everywhere we turn. The presidential election is close, so I join my beautiful friend Allison. We hand out pamphlets door to door and encourage people to go out and vote. Day after day, we reach out. I meet our leader, Sally. I tell her my kids are the Lemonade Stand kids. She lets me know she is meeting with Youngkin for a rally. I boldly ask if I could meet him since he wrote a letter to my kids." She winks. I will see what I can do.

The night is here. We are full of anticipation. The night is windy. We approach the bright home with decorations everywhere. I shake Randy Forbes' hand. I find Sally. Where should we sit? Friends from the past greet us. We saw you on the news. We feel like celebrities. Sally tells us to sit in the front row with the city council. Once we are ready, we will take you into the house to meet Youngkin and Jen Kiggans. My heart is soaring. Randy and others usher us into the house. Who am I that this would happen?

I look around at the pristine room. Pictures of famous people fill the room. The stationery is in a perfect position. The carpet is fresh; the room is filled with honor. They will be here shortly. Jen Kiggans greets us. Oh my gosh! Y'all are famous. Can I get a picture? I smile, not holding back my delight. She sweetly talks to Joshua and Rebecca and recounts what happened.

She is down-to-earth, friendly, and approachable. Anytime you want to visit D.C., let me know, and we can have a tour. Her agent gives me a card. If you need anything, call me. My eyes haze over with the reality of what just happened.

Soon, we get news that Governor Youngkin is approaching. He bends down to get inside the door frame. He is tall and has an honor about him. His friendly talk eases Rebecca and Joshua. Their eyes are wide with wonder. He presents them with an autographed hat. He encourages and praises us for how things have happened with the lemonade stand. I am on cloud nine, and we head to the rest of the rally. Everywhere we go, people

Virginia Governor Glenn Youngkin

remember us from the lemonade stand. I feel like I am in a new family, a new circle that only God could put me in. I leave elated, savoring in what has happened.

Joshua and Rebecca decide to both get 4-wheelers. We research everywhere and we find the perfect ones. A red one for Joshua and a pink one for Rebecca. It is arriving today. The boxes are big, huge, and we tear them open. The kids look, and joy fills their hearts. Never in a million years would I have believed we would have been able to get them 4-wheelers, and here it is. God is restoring all things and giving more than they could ask for.

We have enough money left over to get Busch Gardens passes for the whole family. God once again has answered all of our prayers. Months pass, and we get a phone call: they caught the guy. His name is Estaban, and he has confessed to stealing the money and the jar. We are so relieved, but we also want him to know God's forgiveness and a second chance. He has his court date, and we express wanting him to have leniency. We want a plea deal and not jail time. We ask if he can have community service or a similar alternative. He is a college student who made a bad choice. The court date arrives.

We planned it all out. We have written a letter about forgiveness and how God forgave us. We are ready to read it to him. The kids want to meet him. Everything is ready. We walk into the courtroom. Everything is so official. Rebecca is requested to testify. We wait. Time passes slowly. The courtroom scrambles. Estaban is a no-show. This is bad. He will definitely have a felony charge now. Panic fills the room. Court is cancelled. Our hope and dreams of closure are shattered.

We will call you back when we find him. More weeks have passed. I guess we will just keep praying for him. The lawyer calls me. I wonder what has happened. We have found Estaban. He is in custody right now. You will receive a subpoena in the mail. When it arrives, this time it's only me to testify. Ok, I will be ready. More weeks pass, and excitedly on the other line, "He is willing to take the plea deal." Here are the details: "he will have to do community service for the next year, get a psych evaluation, and do counseling."

He will be on probation during this time. If he does everything right, his charge will drop from a felony to a misdemeanor, and all will be good. This is the best news ever; we don't even have to go back to court! The news does one last report along with the Virginia Pilot and shares about the lesson of forgiveness and how we showed Estaban mercy. God truly tied it all together, and our Lemonade stand story had the best ending ever.

Chapter 60

-The Good, the Bad, and the Scary - Part 1-

Gatlinburg here we come. It is Abigail's big tournament. I am excited to get away with her and Ryan. The weather has not been great. There is flooding nearby. We look out at the hotel room. The water keeps rising. Warnings are given. Be prepared to evacuate. The water was getting dangerously high. The benches down by the river were under water now. Fear begins to rise. Will we be trapped? Hurt? Thankfully, the water begins to go down.

One family makes it across the highway barely before it is closed, and a mudslide happens. We will go around. I feel fear in the air, but finally, we arrive safely back in Virginia. The news is everywhere; the flooding is taking out whole towns. My heart is heavy. I feel burdened for these people, especially after seeing how close we were to the floods. Families are ruined. I pray, but still can't shake the sadness, the hopelessness. Why isn't anyone helping them?

Someone asks me if we are doing any more lemonade stands? Maybe hot cocoa? It can be to help someone. To help give back to North Carolina flood victims! That's it. My kids are willing to do another stand, and I call everyone I can. The desire to help fills my heart. I must do something. I pray God will help this to happen. Wavy 10 wants to cover it again. Thank you, Jesus.

The word is out. We have a short amount of time. Christian Broadcasting Network (CBN) agrees to sponsor the event. Everything is coming together, except how will I get supplies out there? I ask CBN, and they say they can't bring supplies out there right now. There must be someone. My friend Naomi messages me. "I don't know if you need anyone, but I am going to North Carolina this week." Perfect timing. God is so good.

We will have the hot cocoa stand and then give the money to CBN and give supplies to Naomi. Naomi lets me know the stories of families out there without anything. One family has lost everything, and the wife has stage 4 cancer.

My heart aches. I pray, God, what should I do? I can't stop thinking about the families I can help directly. Finally, we have decided that we will give some money to the families. I have everything all together. Many people have given money or supplies to the hot cocoa stand.

One man gives $1,000. We are in shock and awe, and we are so thankful. Blankets, clothing, and pillows are brought. Generosity once again from our amazing community. Though it doesn't compare to the lemonade stand, it is still wonderful. Joshua and Rebecca are learning how to give back. Joy is filling our hearts.

The day is finally here; I bring the money and all the supplies. Bags and bags fill her car. I am overwhelmed once again at God's goodness. All is well, except one thing. This cough. It won't go away. Naomi looks concerned, "Your cough sounds pretty bad; you might want to get it looked at." I try to let it go and whisk away, focused again on the good that just happened.

The cough is still here. It has been weeks, now months. Nothing works. Nothing makes the cough stop. I feel miserable. I hate being sick. Fine, we will go to urgent care. I have not been to the doctor in five years, so this is as good as it gets.

I walk in. Oh, that old familiar feeling catches me. My mind races back to the doctor's office. No, they are going to check my blood pressure. My body begins to tremor. The nurse approaches me with the oxygen meter. My heart starts pounding. I know it's high. Let's take your blood pressure. I try to calm my nerves. Look at this picture, she begins taking my blood pressure. Her eyes widen, "Your blood pressure is elevated. Not as high as your husband's, but it is still high." Why can't I overcome this stupid fear? I am locked in a cycle that I cannot break.

The room is small and rigid. I can't get comfortable. The doctor abruptly comes in. Your lungs sound good, but I am concerned about how long you have had your cough. We will do X-rays just in case. I make my way to the machine. I breathe in and out. Stand forward, arms up. We finish, and it feels like we are waiting forever. The doctor comes in a cheery disposition; your X-rays look normal. You are both free to go. Hoping this medicine works, we are released. Relief calms my body.

Well, I do not want to do that again for a very long time. This is a good Sunday, and worth missing church for peace, knowing all is well. My cough still lingers, won't leave. I sit in my car, stretching my lungs, trying to catch my breath still. I am sure it will get better. It's now Thursday, and I am teaching class. When I finish teaching, Sam lets me know he has to work early today. I get in the car to bring him to work.

I rush to get Sam to work early today. My phone rings. Why is the Now clinic calling me? "Hello, Mrs. Caldwell? "Yes," I say, wondering why they are calling. "The radiologist has found a mass in your right lung." "Wait, what? What do you mean?" She repeats her response with little emotion, "You have a mass in your lung, and you need to go to your PCP doctor and have a CT scan done."

My breath is taken away. "Is this urgent? Do I need to see someone right away?" She replies, "Yes, the sooner the better." I manage a quiet, "Thank you." I hang up. My eyes meet Sam's. With confusion, I say, "They found a mass in my lung." His eyes are gripped with concern. "Are you having trouble breathing?" "Well, yes, but I didn't think that was why." I pull up to Chick-fil-A and I tell him it's probably fine. I will be ok. He slowly shuts the door and enters his work.

Panic fills my heart. My heart was already pounding when she called. I feel trapped in my own body. I call Ryan. I begin to hyperventilate. He says, "I am sure it is fine. You are ok." He tries to comfort me, but nothing is working. I still must drive. I call Brenda from co-op, "Brenda, I, umm."

The words won't come out. I begin sobbing. "I can't breathe," I say with panic in my voice. "What is it?" she asks, concern filling her voice. "Annetta, slow down, I can't understand you." "The radiologist called me. They found a mass in my lung. "Oh no, she quietly says.

"Annetta, I am so sorry. Where are you?" I say, "I am driving. I need to get back there." Her words echoing, "Ok, when you get here, let me know, and I can come to your car with you." Anxiety is ripping my entire being. I can't keep it together. The words echo through my head. We found a mass in your lung. Am I going to die? Do I have cancer? I make it to the co-op.

I stop the car. I have to make it inside. The walk is long; I try to be strong. I open the door and there are my friends. Betty, with a big smile, looks straight into my eyes. "Hey, Annetta, how are you? The words trail off. The words won't come. She hurriedly comes to me. Let's go in here. The leader's room is inviting, warm, and cozy. She holds me as my panic won't stop. Breathe with me. Easy. Slow breaths. You are ok. I am here. Tell me what happened. The words come quickly, almost inaudibly off my lips.

The radiologist said he found a mass in my lung. Tammy, trying to calm me, says ok and she prays. Afterwards, she says, "You do need to go to the doctor to get that looked at." Samantha, one of my best friends, finds me crying with Tammy.

Samantha looks into my eyes, "Annetta, you were made for this. "You have got this." Our eyes lock. She begins telling me I will be ok. And reminds me, if the worst-case scenario does happen, you will have heaven. It's true, I say, but I don't want to die right now. "I know, but there's a reason, and God has got you."

She prays for peace and grace, and that I can miraculously get in to see my doctor. My breathing slows. I am blindsided, though.

I take the first step. I call my doctor. I explain my situation with desperation in my voice. "I know I haven't seen the doctor in five years, but please can he see me?" Her voice is steady, "He isn't taking new patients right now." Panic fills my heart. "Is there anything you can do? The radiologist found a mass in my lung, and I don't trust any other doctor. Can you please ask?" Reluctantly, she says, "I will ask, but I just don't think he can." I wait. I try to talk to others about other things.

My mind constantly races back and forth, rehashing the news. I can't hide my feelings. My other friend Nina finds me. "Hey Annetta, a grin turns south. "What is wrong? What is going on? I tell her, tears streaming down my face. The doctors found a mass in my lung. "I just found out. "NO, she says. This isn't going to happen." She prays. She hugs me. As a warrior in the spirit, she rebukes the enemy.

The phone rings, "Hi, Mrs. Caldwell. I just want you to know, Dr. P has decided to see you as a new patient." My heart leaps for joy. She continues, "We can see you next week." The appointment is set. The first answer to prayer has begun. I tell my friends. They rejoice at the first victory. My other friend, Leona, finds me. She is like a warrior mama for me. "Annetta, don't give up." Fight this. You have to fight this. I can tell you all the things to take."

She prays and asks Jesus to help. To be with me. The room swirls with emotion. She has been with me many times through hard times. I have called her at crazy times. She is a prayer warrior and has been there for me. Abigail approaches me. "Mom, are you ok? What is happening? My friends said they saw you come in very upset." I look at her with serious eyes. "Abigail, they have found a mass in my lung." I can't hold back the tears.

She softly says, "I am sorry, as she barely gets it out. "I don't know what to say." I try to hide my fear. "I will be okay. Everything is ok." My lack of confidence is apparent.

We make it home, and finally, Ryan is there. He hugs me. My body relaxes from the tense and impossible day. We call everyone we can to let them know. I call Veronica. She prays. She helps calm me down. But deep inside, I know the moment is here. What I always feared has come knocking on my door, and it is pushing its way inside.

I talk to Bobby, the campus pastor. Yes, of course, we will pray and would love to have all the Elders from the church to lay hands on you this weekend. Through it all, I am feeling a little less alone. The realization hits me. Tomorrow is the Christmas parade, and Joshua, Becca, Ryan, and I were asked to be VIPs in the parade. It is a huge deal. They are to ride their 4-wheelers while Ryan and I walk. I am still coughing. The weather is freezing, and I might have lung cancer. Is this a good idea? But I can't let them down, I think to myself. God help me.

Though still coughing and struggling, I help prepare for the parade. The kids are so excited. They can't wait to be in the parade. This is the chance of a lifetime. I don't tell them my news. I don't want them to be sad. We drive to the parking lot. The air is crisp and cold. The anticipation is in the air. After hours of sitting and walking around, it's finally time. The parade moves.

We make it to the street. I see a crowd of people everywhere I turn. Joy is in the air. Earlier, I heard my name. "Annetta!" She knows about the mass, and her shout appears to encourage me.

I raise my hands. I wave. I pretend to be happy. But the nagging thoughts are racing towards me. What if I die? What if this is it? Things in life don't seem as big anymore. Numbness tries to hide its ugly place in my heart. Keep pushing through. We make it to the end. My kids' smiles are bigger than I have ever seen.

We prepare for church. People have been praying, but my heart is heavy. I am scared. We enter the building. I go to my spot to worship. I try to worship, but it's harder today. How do I worship knowing that something is wrong with me? I go into the bathroom. A lady greets me. I begin crying. My back bends over, again unable to catch my breath. "Not today. This is not going to happen. She begins praying over me. Peace fills me.

Chapter 61
-The Good, the Bad, and the Scary - Part 2-

God is showing up everywhere I go. And today, with tears in my eyes, I will still worship. Who is coming over here? Jenny, another prayer warrior, comes to me. Her words go deep. She prophesies that God was putting me in a puddle, and I was going to splash it on everyone. That his spirit would just be all over me and splashing onto others. The words are like balm to my hurting heart, and she doesn't even know about the diagnosis.

Ryan and I sit in the back on the floor during the sermon. The Pastor is sharing about whether it's a bad doctor's report. Everything is hitting me. Tears fill my eyes. Hide me, God. I feel so uncovered, so exposed. The campus pastor isn't mentioning the elders praying for me. I guess I will just get someone to pray for me.

With Ryan holding my hand, I move my way through the crowd, trying not to look at anyone, as I feel as if I will burst into tears. The Pastor finds me, "Annetta, great that you are here. Can we still pray over you? I have gathered the elders to pray." Yes, I nod. The circle surrounds me.

His words echo. Is he talking about me? The doctors found a 10 MM mass in her right lung. She has her CT scan on Tuesday. Let's pray God heals her. The prayers begin. I hear it loud in the back. "You will not die but live." The Lord is with you. The prayers are powerful. They have all their hands on me, praying fervently for healing. Tabitha, my friend, prays that the fire of God will burn this mass up.

The words feel like fire in my heart as she speaks. I feel something. I receive all the prayers. Yes, Jesus, yes, heal me. My eyes are swollen from all the crying. God is going to heal you. Fear is cast out. The Pastor prays and lifts me in prayer again. Someone also prays for me to be used by God at these appointments. Maybe I am going through this to help someone else. I am so thankful for all of them. My heart is more at peace with this unknown path before me, and I leave service encouraged, full of hope, yet still nervous.

I must get out of bed. I don't want to. I was at peace yesterday, but reality is hitting me today. I feel as if I am watching my life through a movie. It doesn't feel like real life. The little things don't bother me as much. I hug my kids. I am a little softer and a little more present, not knowing what will happen. I know God is working in all of this, especially since I got a CT scan scheduled right before my doctor's appointment.

The path is laid out for me. I cry again. My family is worried about me. They are praying for me, too. I feel it when I call my sister. Worry is in her voice. I hardly do anything, and there it is. I am lying in my closet, and I feel a peace that makes no sense. Jesus is so close to me. Trust him. But God, it's not supposed to be like this. I am supposed to be enjoying life, pregnant. I thought I would be pregnant before the end of the year, and instead, I am possibly fighting cancer. Everything is happening so fast.

Tuesday is here. What if I react to the dye? What if my body is riddled with cancer? What if? What if? What if? I drop my kids off at the co-op and come in. Slowly. Cautiously. I do not want the wrong thing to be spoken to me. It's like I am afraid of someone speaking careless words. I walk through the doors. Eyes penetrate me. "Hi", I try to talk. I sit at the table with my friends. I can't do this. Nicki has been through cancer. She has been through the scary. "Do you want to pray?" she softly asks. "Yes, I quietly say, barely getting the words out. We find a place to talk.

I find solace in speaking in a safe space. She quietly listens as I bare my soul. I am scared, Nicki. I don't know what will happen. This isn't how things were supposed to go. "I know, sweet friend." We pray and pray. I feel like the Holy Spirit is with me. I see one of my closest friends, Samantha. She hugs me tightly. "You are going to be ok; you got this." I feel so much love. No one is careless. Exact opposite. Everyone is speaking or listening carefully.

Co-op ends, and I head home with the kids. I know tomorrow is the big day. I am busy taking care of the kids, but I know that tomorrow everything can change. It is hard to sleep. I don't want to do this, but I know I have to. When I awake, I have some peace, but fear is mixed in. We head to the car. "I don't know if I can do this," I say, downtrodden. Ryan leans in close, "You can do this." You got this, and God's got you."

The car ride is quiet. We finally arrive at the CT Scan center. I don't hesitate. I must go now, or I won't go at all. I walk quickly through the parking lot. Ryan rushes behind me.

I open the door. The building is fresh and beautiful. There are plants in the center of the waiting area. I try to calm my nerves. I slowly approach the desk. Tears form. Fear is overpowering me. She looks concerned. "You will be ok." Can my husband come back with me? Well, it depends on the technician. We wait for what feels like hours, and the door finally opens. "Annetta Caldwell?" My heart begins to pound. "Can my husband come back with me? "I am so sorry, but no, only you."

My heart sinks. I take off all the jewelry and put on the gown. It's just me in here. The changing room is sterile and small. I come out, greeted by the tech. Her warm smile is comforting, but it doesn't stop my tears from falling. "What's wrong, she asks with a motherly tone. I speak fast, "I am so scared of getting this done. What if I react to the dye? My heart is beating out of my chest. "If anything happens, we will know right away, and we have a doctor on call. "What would he do? He would come check your vitals and take care of you." I look at the large circular machine. My name is across the top. It seems to be yelling, "ANNETTA CALDWELL!"

Never in a million years would I see myself here. I lay down on the soft bed. "They found a 10 mm mass in my lung, I say in between tears." "Oh", she tries to hide her concern. "We are going to put an IV in. No dye, just liquid to start." She begins, and I think I'm okay. I look at her courageously, "Can you pray for me?" Taken aback, she exclaims, "Me, pray for you? I do not usually pray out loud and for others."

As I lift my arms and lay them behind my head, resting on the pillow, I again say, "Yes, uh huh. I would like you to pray." Her prayer starts quietly, "Please be with this lady. Please give those around her grace during this hard road she might be having to travel. Bring your healing to her....she stops.

She almost jumps away, "I can't do this." She is visibly upset. She walks away with me lying on the table. Bewildered, my eyes scan the room. She comes back, "I am so sorry, and begins to pray again. She steps back a second time and reveals a cancer support shirt under her medical shirt. "You had cancer? I ask curiously. "No, my aunt did and died last year. And my mother has had breast cancer three times and is in remission." I see now why I am here, I think to myself.

I feel she is comforted by praying for me, and I believe God has me here for her. "Shall we begin?" My mind rushes back to the procedure. With compassion, she looks towards me, "You know what I am going to do? If you like, I can put you through the machine without dye first and then with dye after." I feel so much better. She moves me slowly towards the machine. The sound is loud and daunting. "Hold your breath."

Breathe normally—direction after direction. Finally, we are done. Ok, not too bad. "Are you ready for the dye?" I feel as if I am ready to jump off a cliff, yet I know I must do this. "Ok, let's do this," I say almost bravely. She gently jokes again, "You will feel like you are peeing in your pants. My heart beats fast. Please, Lord, no reaction. The sensation hits. "I feel like I just peed my pants!" "Yes, it's normal. Your body is reacting perfectly." The machine is taking more pictures. Now I am done.

As I get out, I hug her and thank her. I make my way out of the building. Now the waiting begins. Tomorrow, I will find out everything. As the next day comes, I wonder why I offered to teach my science class this week. It was probably for a distraction. Something shifts in me. As I enter the building, I pull my phone out and play "Good day" by Forrest Frank. A little pep in my step is what I needed. I see Stephanie as I am blasting the music through the hall. "Yes, she yells! Don't waste a bit of your life or your lungs! Praise him!" I surprisingly have some joy. I make it through my class by God's grace. As I walk my way to the round table, reality hits again—fear of the unknown.

My other friend looks at me and begins crying at the news. I can't handle all the emotions. This is the last day of co-op before Christmas break, and I can't find my joy. Everyone around me is happy, celebrating, and I feel jealous. I feel jealous that they have happy, carefree lives. I know they have problems, but do they have these kinds of problems? My heart is torn. My friends gather around me. "Even if it is cancer, you will walk through it. There will be a grace to go through it.

Ryan picks me up. I decide I will go into this appointment bravely. We arrive, and while in the car, I play "Good day" again. This time, I declare it. "NO matter what they say. It's going to be a good day." We enter the waiting room. I try to make jokes, but inside, the nerve-wracking wait is getting harder. The room is almost empty. The TVs are playing in the waiting room. Any moment, they will call me back. "Annetta Caldwell?" My heart skips a beat. Let's check your weight and height. Ok, ok. I begin the long walk to the room.

As I sit, tears come out. I can't stop them. "Is it cancer, I blurt out. The nurse says, "Hold on. Let me check. "No, you don't have cancer." I would have called you earlier. "I don't have cancer?" My heart bursts with joy. Ryan, holding me tight, rejoices too. What about the 10 mm mass? "I don't see it here. Did you get it done at Patient First or one of those clinics?" she asks suspiciously. "No, I got it with your clinic. She looks away and becomes quiet. "Then, no, I don't know." Relief is an understatement.

The doctor comes in and says we don't see the mass, only a few little, tiny ones, and you can see a Pulmonologist in a year or so—nothing of concern. I ask him about every ailment. Every concern, and we agree to do blood work on the spot to double-check everything. Could this be real? I leave with a new hope—a new faith. Right away, I call Veronica. "They can't find the mass! It's gone! "What? That's amazing.

She begins crying on the phone. That's excellent news, Annetta. Praise God! I call the pastor and let him know what happened. He praises God, too. This is the best news person after person, I call, and as the tears of joy and relief hit, I am in awe that God answered this prayer. Thank you, Jesus!

From start to finish, it was one week. I ask the campus pastor if I can share on Sunday. He gets back and says, "Yes! I think it would be an encouragement to the congregation." I constantly tell everyone what happened. I go from elation and joy to weeping. God has done it. What a wonderful early Christmas present. Sunday is here. What a difference from last Sunday. The campus pastor mentions testimonies, and we have one today for you all to hear. "Annetta, come on up."

I begin the story. The radiologist found a 10 mm mass in my right lung. The congregation is quiet. I begin to share how people prayed, and I went to the doctor, and they couldn't find it. It was gone. The congregation starts clapping. It was as if a roar of thanksgiving and praise erupted. I made my way down, feeling the blessings all around me. God did it. God healed me. God is so faithful. I did not even need surgery.

I get a phone call, more good news. The other church asks, "Would you dance at our Christmas Eve Service?" I get to end the year off with a dance. A dance between me and Jesus. A dance of a life that was redeemed and that can share what God can do with a life given to him.

Dancing for the Christmas Eve Service

Conclusion

God is good even when things do not make sense. Sometimes we go through things in life that make us feel like we are breaking. We don't understand why we go through what we do. My heart in sharing my story is to show you that no matter what you go through, God is with you. He will never leave you. He is so loving and so faithful.

If he can take a broken life like mine and make something beautiful out of it, he can do the same for you. Though we are still waiting for some of the promises to come through, I know God will answer them. We are all on a journey of faith. Sometimes easy. Sometimes hard, but we wait. And if we wait, we will see something we never thought we would, God writing our story for him.

Psalm 91: Whoever dwells in the shelter of the Most High will dwell in the shadow of the Almighty. I will say of the Lord my refuge and my fortress, my God, in whom I trust." Surely, he will save you from the fowler's snare and from the deadly pestilence. He will cover you with his feathers, and under his wings you will find refuge; his faithfulness will be your shield and rampart. (NIV)

Psalm 23: The Lord is my shepherd; I shall not want. He makes me lie down in green pastures. He leads me beside the still waters. He restores my soul. He leads me in paths of righteousness for His name's sake. Even though I walk through the valley of the shadow of death, I will fear no evil, for You are with me; Your rod and Your staff, they comfort me. (NIV)

www.ingramcontent.com/pod-product-compliance
Lightning Source LLC
Chambersburg PA
CBHW050253010526
44107CB00003B/306